BARRON'S
STUDENTS' #1 CHOICE

PASS KEY
TO THE
GMAT
GRADUATE MANAGEMENT ADMISSION TEST

Sixth Edition

Eugene D. Jaffe, MBA, Ph.D.
Head, MBA Programs
Ruppin Academic Center
School of Social Sciences and Management

and

Stephen Hilbert, Ph.D.
Professor of Mathematics
Ithaca College

BARRON'S EDUCATIONAL SERIES, INC.

All inquiries should be addressed to:
Barron's Educational Series, Inc.
250 Wireless Boulevard
Hauppauge, New York 11788
www.barronseduc.com

ISBN-13: 978-0-7641-3999-4
ISBN-10: 0-7641-3999-1

ISSN: 1943-6726

PRINTED IN THE UNITED STATES OF AMERICA
9 8 7 6 5 4 3 2 1

CONTENTS

PREFACE

How ready are you for the computer-adaptive Graduate Management Admission Test (GMAT CAT)? How familiar are you with the sorts of questions the exam contains? Do you know what level of mathematical and grammatical ability is necessary to get a high score on the GMAT? Do you have the computer skills you'll need for success? This book will provide you with strategies, review, and practice for taking the actual test. Since the results of the GMAT are used by many graduate schools of business as a means for measuring the qualifications of their applicants, it is important that you do as well as you can on this exam. Your admission to graduate business school may well depend on it.

This book describes in detail the question types found on the GMAT CAT exam. It offers you invaluable advice on how to prepare for the exam, including a step-by-step program designed to help you discover and correct weak points.

If you have scored well on the sample tests in this book, you may take the actual exam with confidence. If this book has shown that you need further practice, then you may wish to begin working with *Barron's Graduate Management Admission Test*, complete with CD-ROM to simulate actual test-taking conditions. The most complete GMAT study guide available, it covers all areas on the test with explanations and numerous practice exercises. The book/CD-ROM package features a diagnostic test and several full-length model exams with answer analyses and self-scoring charts, as well as computer-adaptive tests that allow you to tackle progressively difficult questions as you develop your test-taking proficiency.

ACKNOWLEDGMENTS

The authors gratefully acknowledge the permission to reprint passages.

Pages 152–153 Joseph A. Wraight, *Our Dynamic World: A Survey of Modern Geography.* © 1996 by Joseph A. Wraight. Reprinted with permission of Chilton Book Company.

Pages 156–157 Jean Hollander, "Cops and Writers," *The American Scholar*, Vol. 49, No. 2, Spring 1980. © 1980 by the author. Reprinted with the permission of *The American Scholar*.

Pages 205–206 Committee for Economic Development, Improving Executive Development in the Federal Government. © 1964 by the Committee for Economic Development. Reprinted with the permission of the Committee for Economic Development.

Pages 212–213 Irwin Polishook, "Open Admission Assessed: The Example of the City University of New York, 1970–1975," *Midstream* (April 1976). © The Theodor Herzl Foundation. Reprinted with the permission of the Theodor Herzl Foundation.

Pages 216–217 "The Brains Business," *The Economist.* © 2006 *The Economist.* Reprinted with the permission of *The Economist.*

AT-A-GLANCE
CHECKLIST FOR THE GMAT CAT

BASIC STRATEGIES

1. *Be prepared.* Make sure you practice taking a computer-adaptive test (CAT) ahead of time so you don't waste time during the actual GMAT.
2. *Budget your time.* Calculate the time you may spend on each question.
3. *Read questions carefully.* Make sure you answer the questions that are asked. Consider *all* choices. Remember you must pick the *best* choice, not just a good choice.
4. *Make sure you have clicked on the letter corresponding to your answer.* Once you've confirmed your answer, you cannot go back to that question.
5. *Make educated guesses.* You must answer every question in the CAT, so study the guessing tips in this book.
6. *Get plenty of rest before the exam.* The GMAT exam takes over four hours. Try to get as much rest as possible before the exam.

THE FINER POINTS

Reading Comprehension Questions test your ability to understand *main points* and *significant details* contained in material you have read, and your ability to draw inferences from this material. Tactics to use:

1. Identify the central theme of the passage.
2. Organize mentally how the passage is put together and determine how each part is related to the whole.
3. Determine the opinion or viewpoint that the writer wants the reader to follow or assume.

Sentence Correction Questions test your understanding of the basic rules of English grammar and usage. Tactics to use:

1. Read the sentence carefully, paying more attention to the <u>underlined</u> part.
2. Assume any part of the sentence that is *not* underlined is correct.
3. Verb and pronoun errors are the most common examples—check for these first.
4. Other common errors include misuse of adjectives and adverbs.

Critical Reasoning Questions test your ability to evaluate an assumption, inference, or argument. Each question has five possible answers. Your task is to evaluate each of the five possible choices and select the one that is the best alternative. Tactics to use:

1. Read the question and then read the passage.
2. Learn to spot the major critical reasoning question types.
3. Look for the conclusion first.
4. Find the premises.
5. Do not be opinionated.
6. Do not be intimidated by unfamiliar subjects.

Problem Solving Questions test your ability to work with numbers and require a basic knowledge of arithmetic, algebra, and geometry. Tactics to use:

1. Use educated guesses on questions you can't figure out in two or three minutes.
2. Budget your time so you can concentrate on each question in the test.
3. Try to answer questions by *estimating* or doing a rough calculation.
4. Make sure your answer is in the units asked for.
5. Remember that the more answers you can eliminate, the better your chance of guessing correctly when time is running out.

Data Sufficiency Questions test your reasoning ability. Like the Problem Solving questions, they require a basic knowledge of arithmetic, algebra, and geometry. Each Data Sufficiency question consists of a mathematical problem and two statements containing information relating to it. You must decide whether the problem can be solved by using information from: (A) the first statement alone, but not the second statement alone; (B) the second statement alone, but not the first statement alone; (C) both statements together, but neither alone; or (D) either of the statements alone. Choose (E) if the problem cannot be solved, even by using both statements together.

Tactics

1. Don't waste time figuring out the exact answer.
2. Use the strategies in Chapter 5 to make intelligent guesses if you can't answer the questions.

1

AN INTRODUCTION TO THE GMAT CAT

The most productive approach to undertaking the actual study and review necessary for any examination is first to determine the answers to some basic questions: What? Where? When? and How? In this case, what is the purpose of the Graduate Management Admission Test (GMAT)? What does it measure? Where and when is the exam given? And most important, how can you prepare to demonstrate aptitude and ability to study business at the graduate level?

The following discussion centers on the purpose behind the Graduate Management Admission Test and answers basic questions about the general format and procedure used on the computer-adaptive GMAT.

THE PURPOSE OF THE GMAT

The purpose of the GMAT is to measure your ability to think systematically and to employ the verbal and mathematical skills that you have acquired throughout your years of schooling. The types of questions that are used to test these abilities are discussed in the next chapter. It should be noted that the test does not aim to measure your knowledge of specific business or academic subjects. No specific business experience is necessary, nor will any specific academic subject area be covered. You are assumed to have knowledge of basic algebra (but not calculus), geometry, and arithmetic, and of the basic conventions of standard written English.

In effect, the GMAT provides business school admission officers with an objective measure of academic abilities to supplement subjective criteria used in the selection process, such as interviews, grades, and references. Suppose you are an average student in a college with high grading standards. Your overall grade average may be lower than that of a student from a college with lower grading standards. The GMAT allows you and the other student to be tested under similar conditions using the same grading standard. In this way, a more accurate picture of your all-around ability can be established.

WHERE TO APPLY

Information about the exam can be found on the GMAT's official website.

Unlike the pencil and paper GMAT exam, which was scheduled on fixed dates four times a year, the computer-adaptive test may be taken three weeks per month, six days a week, ten hours a day at 400 testing centers in the United States and Canada and major cities throughout the world. The test-taker will be seated in a testing alcove with only a few others present at the same time and can register for a test a few days before a preferred time. To schedule a test, simply call the ETS toll-free number 1-800-717-GMAT (within the United States and Canada only) or online at *http://www.mba.com*. Payment may be made by credit card, check, or money order. It is wise to schedule your exam early to ensure that the schools to which you are applying receive your scores in time.

THE TEST FORMAT

The GMAT CAT contains questions of the following types: Analytical Writing, Reading Comprehension, Problem Solving, Data Sufficiency, Critical Reasoning, and Sentence Correction. In the past, exams have included Analysis of Situations questions, but these questions have now been replaced by questions on Critical Reasoning.

WHAT IS A COMPUTER-ADAPTIVE TEST (CAT)?

In a computer-adaptive test, each question is shown on a personal computer screen one at a time. On the test, questions are of high, medium, and low difficulty. The first question on a test is of medium difficulty; the relative difficulty of the next question depends on your answer to the first question. If you answered correctly, the next question will be of greater difficulty. If your answer was incorrect, the next question will be less difficult, and so on. However, the choice of subsequent questions is not only based on whether the preceding answer was correct or incorrect, but also on the difficulty level of the preceding question, whether previous questions have covered a variety of question types, and specific test content. This procedure is repeated for each of your answers. In this way, the CAT adjusts questions to your ability.

The computer-adaptive GMAT will have three parts: a writing section which consists of writing two essays, a quantitative test, and a verbal test.

You will have 30 minutes to write each essay.

The quantitative test will be composed of Problem Solving and Data Sufficiency type questions. There will be 37 questions and you will have 75 minutes to finish this section.

The verbal test will be composed of Reading Comprehension, Critical Reasoning, and Sentence Correction type questions. There will be 41 questions and you will have 75 minutes to finish this section.

There is an optional five-minute break between each section of the exam.

You can download free test tutorials from *www.mba.com*. These will help you to review the basic skills of taking a computer-adaptive test, such as entering answers and accessing HELP. You should review these procedures before you arrive at the test center, because any time that you use to review HELP screens will mean less time for you to work on the test questions.

It is possible that your tests may contain some experimental questions. These questions may or may not be labeled experimental. You should do your best on any question that is not labeled experimental. Experimental questions are **not** counted in your scores.

In the GMAT CAT, once you enter and confirm your answer you **cannot** change the answer. You can't go back and work on previous questions if you finish a section early. Furthermore, you must answer each question before you can see the next question. (You will not be able to skip any questions.)

YOU'VE ANSWERED THE FIRST QUESTION: WHAT'S NEXT?

Suppose that you answered that first question correctly and then get a more difficult one that you also answer correctly and then an even harder one that you answer incorrectly. Will you get a lower score than say a candidate that answers the first question incorrectly and then gets an easier one that is answered correctly? No, because difficult questions are worth more points than easier ones. So, in the end, the mixture of questions that each candidate gets should be balanced to reflect his or her ability and performance. There is little possibility that a candidate will have a higher score because he or she answered more easy questions correctly.

These rules apply to both the quantitative (problem solving and data sufficiency) and qualitative (reading comprehension, sentence correction, and critical reasoning) multiple-choice type questions. The Analytical Writing Assessment (AWA), described in Chapter 6, will be written using the computer, but it will not be adaptive. Test-takers will write essays in response to two questions as was the case in the paper and pencil test. The overall quality of your thinking and writing will be evaluated by faculty members from a number of academic disciplines, including management. It will also be rated by an automated essay scoring system, developed by ETS, called an e-rater™. After extensive testing, the e-rater™ system was found to have a 92% agreement with human readers, which is about the same rate at which two human readers agree.

Another fact about the CAT is that questions cannot be skipped. You must answer the present question in order to proceed to the next one. This means that if you do not know the answer, you must guess (tips for guessing are given on page 8.) Answering a question means entering your choice by clicking the mouse next to the alternative you have chosen and then clicking on the "confirm" icon. Once you have confirmed your answer, you cannot go back to check.

IMPORTANCE OF THE GMAT

Your score on the GMAT is only one of the several factors examined by admissions officers. Your undergraduate record, for example, is at least as important as your GMAT score. Thus, a low score does not mean that no school will accept you, nor does a high GMAT score guarantee acceptance at the school of your choice. However, since your score is one important factor, you should try to do as well as you can on the exam. Using this book should help you to maximize your score.

Most college catalogs do not state what the minimum GMAT requirement is, but the annual reports of most MBA programs do note the average GMAT score of the last incoming student body. This is probably a good indication of the necessary ballpark figure for admission. However, obtaining a score somewhat below that figure does not mean that acceptance is not possible. First of all, it is an average figure. Some scored below, but were accepted.

The GMAT is only one of a number of criteria for admission. Before applying to a college or university, determine what criteria are considered for admission and how these criteria are ranked by order of importance. Directors of MBA programs, admissions officers, college catalogs, and annual reports should provide this information.

HOW TO PREPARE FOR THE GMAT CAT

You should now be aware of the purpose of the GMAT and have a general idea of the format of the test. With this basic information, you are in a position to begin your study and review. The rest of this guide represents a study plan that will enable you to prepare for the GMAT. If used properly, it will help you diagnose your weak areas and take steps to remedy them.

Begin your preparation by becoming as familiar as possible with the various types of questions that appear on the exam. When you feel you understand this material completely, take the Practice Tests that follow and evaluate your results on the self-scoring tables provided at the end of the tests. (An explanation of how to use these tables follows.) A low score in any area indicates that you should spend more time reviewing that particular material. Study the review section for that area until you feel you have mastered it. For best results, try to simulate exam conditions as closely as possible when taking sample tests: no unscheduled breaks or interruptions, strict adherence to time limits, and no use of outside aids.

THE SELF-SCORING TABLES

The Self-Scoring Tables for each sample test in this guide can be used as a means of evaluating your weaknesses in particular subject areas and should help you plan your study program most effectively.

After completing a sample test, turn to the Answers section which immediately follows each test. Determine the number of *correct* answers you had for each section. This is your correct score for that section. Now turn to the section Evaluating Your Score, which follows the Answers Explained section of each test. Record your scores in the appropriate score boxes in the Self-Scoring Table as shown below.

SELF-SCORING TABLE		
Section	Score	Rating
Quantitative	13	Poor
Verbal	27	Good

Use the rating scale to find your rating for each section. A typical rating scale follows.

SELF-SCORING SCALE—RATING				
Section	Poor	Fair	Good	Excellent
Quantitative	0–15	15–25	26–30	31–37
Verbal	0–15	15–25	26–30	31–41

A rating of FAIR or POOR in any area indicates that you need to spend more time reviewing that material.

Next, be familiar with the CAT system. Make sure you know how everything works (e.g., scrolling) before you start the exam. Pace is very important. Losing time because of unfamiliarity with the CAT is avoidable with practice using this manual and other tools.

TEST-TAKING STRATEGIES

1. **The first five or so questions count more than later questions.** Budget a little more time for these questions. You have about 1¾ minutes for each verbal question and 2 minutes for each quantitative question. So, be prepared to spend more time with the initial questions.

2. **Answer as many questions as possible.** While there is no minimum number to answer in order to get a score, your score will be lower if fewer questions are answered.

3. **If you are not sure, guess.** Unlike the former GMAT version, there is no penalty for a wrong answer, so if you are running out of time, guess. Also, since you have to give an answer in order to proceed to the next question, guessing may be necessary. For some tips see the Guessing section that follows.

4. **Pace yourself and be aware of remaining time.** Be aware of the number of questions and remaining time. How much time is left in a test section can be determined by pressing the time icon and a clock will appear on the upper left-hand side of the screen.

5. **Confirm your answer only when you are confident that it is correct.** Remember, you cannot return to a previous question and you must confirm your answer in order to move on to the next question.

6. **Be careful about section exit and test quit commands.** Once you confirm a section exit command you cannot go back. Confirming the test quit command automatically ends the session with no chance of continuing.

GUESSING

Two elements should be considered in addressing the area of guessing. First, consider the way your score is determined by the administrators of the GMAT. If you do not answer a question, you cannot proceed to the next one. So, if you are stuck it helps to guess.

Or, if you are near the end of a test section and time is running out, you have two options. You can guess the answers to questions if you are unsure of the correct answer, or you can quit the section when time runs out. As we pointed out before, it is best to spend more time with the first five questions and less time with the remaining ones. So, guessing becomes an important strategy when time is critical. The probability of selecting the correct answer by random guessing is 1 out of 5, or 0.20, which is rather low. However, suppose that you have had time to read the question and have been able to eliminate two answer alternatives, but are still unsure of the correct answer. Now, a random guess of the correct answer among the remaining alternatives has a probability of 0.33. Obviously, if you are able to eliminate three alternatives, you then have a 50-50 chance of guessing the correct answer. Assuming that time has run out, guessing in this situation is a very low risk.

MANEUVERING THE GMAT CAT PC SCREEN

While you will have the opportunity to try out the so-called "Testing Tools" of the CAT before taking the test, you will have an advantage if you are already familiar with them beforehand. These testing tools consist of a number of icons or commands by which you navigate the test.

Quit Program. If you click this, you terminate the test. Only do this if you have completed the entire test.

Section Exit. Clicking this button terminates a test section and enables you to go on to the next test section.

Time. Clicking this icon will show you how much time (shown in hours, minutes, and seconds) remains on the test.

? Help. Clicking this button will activate the help function. The help function contains directions for the question you are working on, directions for the section you are working on, general directions, how to scroll, and information about the testing tools.

Next and **Answer Confirm.** Both of these buttons work in sequence. When you are sure of your answer, click the *Next* button to move on to the next question. You will then see that the Answer Confirm button will become dark. Clicking it will save your answer and bring the next question to the screen.

You should also practice the word processing tools needed for the Analytical Writing Assessment (AWA).

Page up—moves the cursor up one page.
Page down—moves the cursor down one page.
Backspace—removes the text to the left of the cursor.
Delete—removes text to the right of the cursor.
Home—moves the cursor to the beginning of a line.
End—moves the cursor to the end of a line.
Arrows—move the cursor up, down, left, and right.
Enter—move the cursor to the beginning of the next line.

There are also *Cut, Paste,* and *Undo* functions.

2

READING COMPREHENSION REVIEW

DESCRIPTION OF THE TEST

The Reading Comprehension questions test your ability to analyze written information and include passages from the humanities, the social sciences, and the physical and biological sciences.

The typical Reading Comprehension part of the Verbal section consists of three passages with a total of approximately 15 questions. You will be allowed to scroll through the passages when answering the questions. However, many of the questions may be based on what is *implied* in the passages, rather than on what is explicitly stated. Your ability to draw inferences from the material is critical to successfully completing this section. You are to select the best answer from five alternatives.

TEST-TAKING TIPS

1. Read the passage, noting important points, names, and so on on your scratch paper.
2. Determine the central thought. Is there a topic sentence that expresses the main idea succinctly? What title would you give the passage?
3. Notice the specific details or statements that the writer gives to support the main idea.
4. Note the special techniques used by the author. These may include reasoning from experimental data (inductive method) or from principles accepted in advance (deductive method) and the use of examples, anecdotes, analogies, and comparisons.

11

5. Determine the author's purpose. Is he or she seeking to inform, to persuade, to satirize, to evoke pity, to amuse, to arouse to action?

6. Look at the questions, noting the type of information called for.

7. Pay attention to the wording of each question. A question that begins "The main idea of the passage is..." calls for a different kind of reasoning from a question that begins "Which of the following is mentioned...?" Watch out for questions that specify "All of the following EXCEPT..." or "Which of the following is NOT..." since these phrases mean you should look for the *false* or *inapplicable* answer rather than the *true* one.

8. All reading comprehension questions on the GMAT can be answered on the basis of information provided in the passage. Therefore, don't bring in your own prior knowledge or your personal opinions when answering the questions; they may be inapplicable, inaccurate, or misleading.

9. Read all five answer choices carefully before selecting an answer. Sometimes two or more choices will have elements of truth; however, only one answer will be the best. Don't overlook the best answer by hastily choosing the first choice that seems reasonable.

TYPES OF QUESTIONS

Reading comprehension questions usually fall into several general categories. In most questions, you will be asked about one of the following:

Main Idea. In this type of question you may be asked about the main idea or theme of the passage, about a possible title, or about the author's primary objective. Usually the main idea refers to the passage as a whole, not to some segment or part of the passage. The main idea is typically (but not always) found in the first paragraph. It will be a statement that gives the overall theme of the passage. In many cases, it will be in the form of an argument, including a premise and conclusion.

Supporting Ideas. In this type of question, you may be asked about the idea expressed in one part of the passage, rather than about the passage as a whole. Questions of this type test your ability to distinguish between the main idea and those themes that support it, some of which may be implicit or implied rather than explicitly stated.

Drawing Inferences. Questions of this sort ask about ideas that are not explicitly stated in a passage. These questions refer to meanings implied by the author based on information given in the passage. Typical questions are:

1. The author feels (believes) that...
2. In reference to (event) it may be inferred that...

Specific Details. In this type of question you may be asked about specific facts or details the author has stated explicitly in the passage. This sort of question may take the following forms:

1. Which of the following statements is mentioned by the author?
2. All of the following are given as reasons for ( ) EXCEPT:
3. The author argues that...

Applying Information from the Passage to Other Situations. These questions ask you to make an analogy between a situation described in the passage and a similar situation or event listed in the question. Unlike other types of questions, these describe situations *not* given in the passage, but rather those that are analogous to those in the passage. In order to answer a question of this kind, you must be able to draw a parallel between the situation in the question and its counterpart in the passage.

Tone or Attitude of the Passage. These questions concentrate on the author's style, attitude, or mood. In order to determine this attitude, look for key words, such as adjectives that reveal if the author is "pessimistic," "critical," "supportive," or "objective" about an event, idea, or situation in the passage.

The Logical Structure of the Passage. These types of questions test your understanding of the overall meaning, logic, or organization of a passage. You may be asked how several ideas in a passage are interrelated or how a passage is constructed, classifies, compares, or describes events or situations. You may be asked about the strengths or weaknesses the author is making, to identify assumptions, or to evaluate counterarguments.

Determining the Meaning of Words from the Context. When a question asks for the meaning of a word, it can usually be deduced from the context of the passage. Remember, you are not required to know the meaning of technical or foreign words.

SAMPLE PASSAGE WITH QUESTIONS, ANSWERS, AND ANALYSIS

The following passage will give you an idea of the format of the Reading Comprehension questions. Read the passage through and then answer the questions, making sure to leave yourself enough time to complete them all.

TIME: 10 minutes

Political theories have, in fact, very little more to do with musical creation than electronics theories have. Both merely determine methods of distribution. The exploitation of these methods is subject to political regulation and is quite rigidly
(5) regulated in many countries. The revolutionary parties, both in Russia and elsewhere, have tried to turn composers on to supposedly revolutionary subject-matter. The net result for either art or revolution has not been very important. Neither has official fascist music accomplished much either for music or for
(10) Italy or Germany.

Political party-influence on music is just censorship anyway. Performances can be forbidden and composers disciplined for what they write, but the creative stimulus comes from elsewhere. Nothing really "inspires" an author but money or food or
(15) love.

That persons or parties subventioning musical uses should wish to retain veto power over the works used is not at all surprising. That our political masters (or our representatives) should exercise a certain negative authority, a censorship, over
(20) the exploitation of works whose content they consider dangerous to public welfare is also in no way novel or surprising. But that such political executives should think to turn the musical profession into a college of political theorists or a bunch of hired propagandists is naïve of them. Our musical civilization is older
(25) than any political party. We can deal on terms of intellectual equality with acoustical engineers, with architects, with poets, painters, and historians, even with the Roman clergy if necessary. We cannot be expected to take very seriously the inspirational dictates of persons or of groups who think they can
(30) pay us to get emotional about ideas. They can pay us to get emotional all right. Anybody can. Nothing is so emotion-producing as money. But emotions are factual; they are not generated by ideas. On the contrary, ideas are generated by emotions; and emotions, in turn, are visceral states produced direct-
(35) ly by facts like money and food and sexual intercourse. To have any inspirational quality there must be present facts or immediate anticipations, not pie-in-the-sky.

Now pie-in-the-sky has its virtues as a political ideal, I presume. Certainly most men want to work for an eventual
(40) common good. I simply want to make it quite clear that ideals about the common good (not to speak of mere political necessity) are not very stimulating subject-matter for music. They don't produce visceral movements the way facts do. It is notorious that musical descriptions of hell, which is something
(45) we can all imagine, are more varied and vigorous than the placid banalities that even the best composers have used to describe heaven; and that all composers do better on really present matters than on either: matters like love and hatred and hunting and war and dancing around and around.
(50)   The moral of all this is that the vetoing of objective subject

matter is as far as political stimulation or censorship can go in advance. Style is personal and emotional, not political at all. And form or design, which is impersonal, is not subject to any political differences of opinion.

1. The author is making a statement defending

   I. intellectual freedom
   II. the apolitical stance of most musicians
   III. emotional honesty

  (A) I only   (D) I and III only
  (B) II only   (E) I, II, and III
  (C) I and II only

2. The tone of the author in the passage is

  (A) exacting   (D) optimistic
  (B) pessimistic   (E) fatalistic
  (C) critical

3. The author's reaction to political influence on music is one of

  (A) surprise
  (B) disbelief
  (C) resignation
  (D) deference
  (E) rancor

4. According to the author, political attempts to control the subject matter of music

  (A) will be resisted by artists wherever they are made
  (B) may succeed in censoring but not in inspiring musical works
  (C) will succeed only if the eventual goal is the common good
  (D) are less effective than the indirect use of social and economic pressure
  (E) have profoundly influenced the course of modern musical history

5. The author refers to "musical descriptions of hell" (line 44) to make the point that

(A) musical inspiration depends on the degree to which the composer's imagination is stimulated by his subject

(B) composers are better at evoking negative emotions and ideas than positive ones

(C) music is basically unsuited to a role in support of political tyranny

(D) religious doctrines have inspired numerous musical compositions

(E) political ideals are a basic motivating force for most contemporary composers

6. The author implies that political doctrines usually fail to generate artistic creativity because they are too

(A) naïve

(B) abstract

(C) rigidly controlled

(D) concrete

(E) ambiguous

Answers:

1. **(D)**   2. **(C)**   3. **(C)**   4. **(B)**   5. **(A)**   6. **(B)**

Analysis:

1. **(D)** The author is arguing that musicians will not conform to any control over their creativity. Thus, they want to be intellectually free and emotionally honest. It does not mean that they could not be active in politics (apolitical).

2. **(C)** The author is critical of attempts to censor the arts, especially music.

3. **(C)** The author does not find censorship surprising (lines 18–21), nor does he take it seriously (line 28). He is resigned to attempts at censorship, although he does not believe it can inspire creativity.

4. **(B)** See paragraph 2.
5. **(A)** See lines 43–49.
6. **(B)** See paragraph 4, in which the author states that "ideals" do not inspire music as "facts" do; and also see lines 14–15 and 35–37.

A METHOD OF APPROACH

BASIC READING SKILLS

A primary skill necessary for good reading comprehension is the understanding of the meanings of individual words. Knowledge of a wide and diversified vocabulary enables you to detect subtle differences in sentence meaning that may hold the key to the meaning of an entire paragraph or passage. For this reason, it is important that you familiarize yourself with as many words as possible.

A second reading skill to be developed is the ability to discover the central theme of a passage. By making yourself aware of what the entire passage is about, you are in a position to relate what you read to this central theme, logically picking out the main points and significant details as you go along. Although the manner in which the central theme is stated may vary from passage to passage, it can usually be found in the title (if one is presented), in the "topic sentence" of a paragraph in shorter passages, or, in longer passages, by reading several paragraphs.

A third essential skill is the capacity to organize mentally how the passage is put together and determine how each part is related to the whole. This is the skill you will have to use to the greatest degree on the GMAT, where you must pick out significant and insignificant factors, remember main details, and relate information you have read to the central theme.

In general, a mastery of these three basic skills will provide you with a solid basis for better reading comprehension wherein you will be able to read carefully to draw a conclusion from the material, decide the meanings of words and ideas presented and how they in turn affect the meaning of the passage, and recognize opinions and views that are expressed.

APPLYING BASIC READING SKILLS

The only way to become adept at the three basic reading skills outlined above is to practice using the techniques involved as much as possible. Studying the meanings of new words you encounter in all your reading material will soon help you establish a working knowledge of many words. In the same manner, making an effort to locate topic sentences, general themes, and specific details in material you read will enable you to improve your skills in these areas. The following drills will help. After you have read through them and answered the questions satisfactorily, you can try the longer practice exercise at the end.

FINDING THE TOPIC SENTENCE

The term "topic sentence" is used to describe the sentence that gives the key to an entire paragraph. Usually the topic sentence is found in the beginning of a paragraph. However, there is no absolute rule. A writer may build the paragraph to a conclusion, putting the key sentence at the end. Here is an example in which the topic sentence is located at the beginning:

EXAMPLE 1:
The world faces a serious problem of overpopulation. Right now many people starve from lack of adequate food. Efforts are being made to increase the rate of food production, but the number of people to be fed increases at a faster rate.

The idea is stated directly in the opening sentence. You know that the passage will be about "a serious problem of overpopulation." Like a heading or caption, the topic sentence sets the stage or gets your mind ready for what follows in that paragraph.

Before you try to locate the topic sentence in a paragraph you must remember that this technique depends upon reading and judgment. Read the whole passage first. Then try to decide which sentence comes closest to expressing the main point of the paragraph. Do not worry about the position of the topic sentence in the paragraph; look for the most important statement. Find the idea to which all the other sentences relate.

Try to identify the topic sentence in this passage:

EXAMPLE 2:

During the later years of the American Revolution, the Articles of Confederation government was formed. This government suffered severely from a lack of power. Each state distrusted the others and gave little authority to the central or federal government. The Articles of Confederation produced a government that could not raise money from taxes, prevent Indian raids, or force the British out of the United States.

What is the topic sentence? Certainly the paragraph is about the Articles of Confederation. However, is the key idea in the first sentence or in the second sentence? In this instance, the *second* sentence does a better job of giving you the key to this paragraph—the lack of centralized power that characterized the Articles of Confederation. The sentences that complete the paragraph relate more to the idea of "lack of power" than to the time when the government was formed. Don't assume that the topic sentence is always the first sentence of a paragraph. Try this:

EXAMPLE 3:

There is a strong relation between limited education and low income. Statistics show that unemployment rates are highest among those adults who attended school the fewest years. Most jobs in a modern industrial society require technical or advanced training. The best pay goes with the jobs that demand thinking and decisions based on knowledge. A few people manage to overcome their limited education by personality or a "lucky break." However, studies of lifetime earnings show that the average high school graduate earns more than the average high school dropout, who in turn earns more than the average adult who has not finished eighth grade.

Here, the first sentence contains the main idea of the whole paragraph. One more example should be helpful:

EXAMPLE 4:

They had fewer men available as soldiers. Less than one-third of the railroads and only a small proportion of the nation's industrial production was theirs. For most of the war their coastline was blockaded by Northern ships. It is a tribute to Southern leadership and the courage of the people that they were not defeated for four years.

In this case you will note that the passage builds up to its main point. The topic sentence is the last one. Practice picking out the topic sentences in other material you read until it becomes an easy task.

FINDING THE GENERAL THEME

A more advanced skill is the ability to read several paragraphs and relate them to one general theme or main idea. The procedure involves careful reading of the entire passage and deciding which idea is the central or main one. You can tell you have the right idea when it is most frequent or most important, or when every sentence relates to it. As you read the next passage, note the underlined parts.

EXAMPLE:

True democracy means direct rule by the people. A good example can be found in a modern town meeting in many small New England towns. All citizens aged twenty-one or over may vote. They not only vote for officials, but they also get together to vote on local laws (or ordinances). The small size of the town and the limited number of voters make this possible.

In the cities, voters cast ballots for officials who get together to make the laws. Because the voters do not make the laws directly, this system is called indirect democracy or representative government. There is no problem of distance to travel, but it is difficult to run a meeting with hundreds of thousands of citizens.

Representation of voters and a direct voice in making laws are more of a problem in state or national governments. The numbers of citizens and the distances to travel make representative govern-ment the most practical way to make laws.

Think about the passage in general and the underlined parts in particular. Several examples discuss voting for officials and mak-ing laws. In the first paragraph both of these are done by the vot-ers. The second paragraph describes representative government in which voters elect officials who make laws. The last paragraph emphasizes the problem of size and numbers and says that rep-resentative government is more practical. In the following ques-tion, put all these ideas together.

The main theme of this passage is that
(A) the United States is not democratic
(B) citizens cannot vote for lawmakers
(C) representative government does not make laws
(D) every citizen makes laws directly
(E) increasing populations lead to less direct democracy

The answer is choice (E). Choices (B), (C), and (D) can be eliminated because they are not true of the passage. Choice (A) may have made you hesitate a little. The passage makes com-ments about *less direct* democracy, but it never says that repre-sentative government is *not democratic.*

In summary, in order to find the general theme:
1. Read at your normal speed.
2. Locate the topic sentence in each paragraph.
3. Note ideas that are frequent or emphasized.
4. Find the idea to which most of the passage is related.

FINDING LOGICAL RELATIONSHIPS

In order to fully understand the meaning of a passage, you must first look for the general theme and then relate the ideas and opin-ions found in the passage to this general theme. In this way, you can determine not only what is important but also how the ideas interrelate to form the whole. From this understanding, you will be better able to answer questions that refer to the passage.

As you read the following passages, look for general theme and supporting facts, words, or phrases that signal emphasis or shift in thought, and the relation of one idea to another.

EXAMPLE:
The candidate who wants to be elected pays close attention to statements and actions that will make the voters see him favorably. In ancient Rome candidates wore pure white togas (the Latin word *candidatus* means "clothed in white") to indicate that they were pure, clean, and above any "dirty work." However, it is interesting to note that such a toga was not worn after election.

In more modern history, candidates have allied themselves with political parties. Once a voter knows and favors the views of a certain political party, he may vote for anyone with that party's label. Nevertheless, divisions of opinion develop, so that today there is a wide range of candidate views in any major party.

The best conclusion to be drawn from the first paragraph is that after an election
(A) all candidates are dishonest
(B) candidates are less concerned with symbols of integrity
(C) candidates do not change their ideas
(D) officials are always honest
(E) policies always change

You noted the ideas about a candidate in Rome. You saw the word "however" signal a shift in ideas or thinking. Now the third step rests with your judgment. You cannot jump to a conclusion; you must see which conclusion is reasonable or fair. Choices (A), (D), and (E) should make you wary. They say "all" or "always" which means without exception. The last sentence is not that strong or positive. Choices (B) and (C) must be considered. There is nothing in the paragraph that supports the fact that candidates do not change their ideas. This forces you into choice (B) as the only statement logically related to what the paragraph said.

MAKING INFERENCES

An inference is not stated. It is assumed by the reader from something said by the writer. An inference is the likely or probable conclusion rather than the direct, logical one. It usually involves an opinion or viewpoint that the writer wants the reader to follow or assume. In another kind of inference, the reader figures out the author's opinion even though it is not stated. The clues are generally found in the manner in which facts are presented and in the choice of words and phrases. Opinion is revealed by the one-sided nature of a passage in which no opposing facts are given. It is shown further by "loaded" words that reveal the author's feelings.

It is well worth noting that opinionated writing is often more interesting than straight factual accounts. Some writers are very colorful, forceful, or amusing in presenting their views. You should understand that there is nothing wrong with reading opinions. You should read varied opinions, but know that they are opinions. Then make up your own mind.

Not every writer will insert an opinion obviously. However, you can get clues from how often the same idea is said (frequency), whether arguments are balanced on both sides (fairness), and the choice of wording (emotional or loaded words). Look for the clues in this next passage.

EXAMPLE:

Slowly but surely the great passenger trains of the United States have been fading from the rails. Short-run commuter trains still rattle in and out of the cities. Between major cities you can still find a train, but the schedules are becoming less frequent. The Twentieth Century Limited, The Broadway Limited, and other luxury trains that sang along the rails at 60 to 80 miles an hour are no longer running. Passengers on other long runs complain of poor service, old equipment, and costs in time and money. The long distance traveller today accepts the noise of jets, the congestion at airports, and the traffic between airport and city. A more elegant and graceful way is becoming only a memory.

1. With respect to the reduction of long-run passenger trains, this writer expresses

   (A) regret
   (B) pleasure
   (C) grief
   (D) elation
   (E) anger

Before you choose the answer, you must deduce what the writer's feeling is. He does not actually state his feeling, but clues are available so that you may infer what it is. Choices (B) and (D) are impossible, because he gives no word that shows he is pleased by the change. Choice (C) is too strong, as is choice (E). Choice (A) is the most reasonable inference to make. He is sorry to see the change. He is expressing regret.

2. The author seems to feel that air travel is

   (A) costly   (D) elegant
   (B) slow   (E) uncomfortable
   (C) streamlined

Here we must be careful because he says very little about air travel. However, his one sentence about it presents three negative or annoying points. The choice now becomes fairly clear. Answer (E) is correct.

PRACTICE EXERCISE WITH ANSWERS AND ANALYSIS

Time: 9 minutes

Directions: This part contains a reading passage. You are to read it carefully. When answering the questions, you *will* be able to refer to the passages. The questions are based on what is *stated* or *implied* in the passage. You have nine minutes to complete this part.

Above all, colonialism was hated for its explicit assumption that the civilizations of colonized peoples were inferior. Using

slogans like *The White Man's Burden* and *La Mission Civilica-*
trice, Europeans asserted their moral obligation to impose their
(5) way of life on those endowed with inferior cultures. This orientation was particularly blatant among the French. In the
colonies, business was conducted in French. Schools used
that language and employed curricula designed for children in
France. One scholar suggests that Muslim children probably
(10) learned no more about the Maghreb than they did about Austra-
lia. In the Metropole, intellectuals discoursed on the weakness
of Arab-Islamic culture. A noted historian accused Islam of
being hostile to science. An academician wrote that Arabic—the
holy language of religion, art, and the Muslim sciences—is
(15) "more of an encumbrance than an aid to the mind. It is absolutely
devoid of precision." There was of course an element of truth in
the criticisms. After all, Arab reformists had been engaging
in self-criticism for decades. Also, at least some Frenchmen
honestly believed they were helping the colonized. A Resident
(20) General in Tunisia, for example, told an assemblage of Muslims
with sincerity, "We shall distribute to you all that we have of
learning; we shall make you a party to everything that makes for
the strength of our intelligence." But none of this could change
or justify the cultural racism in colonial ideologies. To the
(25) French, North Africans were only partly civilized and could be
saved only by becoming Frenchmen. The reaction of the colonized was of course to defend their identity and to label colonial
policy, in the words of Algerian writer Malek Hadad, "cultural
asphyxia." Throughout North Africa, nationalists made the
(30) defense of Arabo-Islamic civilization a major objective, a value
in whose name they demanded independence. Yet the crisis of
identity, provoked by colonial experiences, has not been readily
assured and lingers into the post-colonial period. A French
scholar describes the devastating impact of colonialism by
(35) likening it to "the role played for us (in Europe) by the doctrine
of original sin." Frantz Fanon, especially in his *Studies in a Dying
Colonialism,* well expresses the North African perspective.

Factors producing militant and romantic cultural nationalism are anchored in time. Memories of colonialism are already *(40)* beginning to fade and, when the Maghreb has had a few decades in which to grow, dislocations associated with social change can also be expected to be fewer. Whether this means that the cultural nationalism characteristic of the Maghreb today will disappear in the future cannot be known. But a preoccupation *(45)* with identity and culture and an affirmation of Arabism and Islam have characterized the Maghreb since independence and these still remain today important elements in North African life.

A second great preoccupation in independent North Africa is the promotion of a modernist social revolution. The countries *(50)* of the Maghreb do not pursue development in the same way and there have been variations in policies within each country. But all three spend heavily on development. In Tunisia, for example, the government devotes 20–25% of its annual budget to education, and literacy has climbed from 15% in 1956 to about *(55)* 50% today. A problem, however, is that such advances are not always compatible with objectives flowing from North African nationalism. In Morocco, for instance, when the government decided to give children an "Arab" education, it was forced to limit enrollments because, among other things, most Moroc- *(60)* cans had been educated in French and the country consequently had few teachers qualified to teach in Arabic. Two years later, with literacy rates declining, this part of the Arabization program was postponed. The director of Arabization declared, "We are not fanatics; we want to enter the modern world."

1. Which of the following titles best describes the content of the passage?

(A) *Education in the Levant*

(B) *Nationalism in North Africa*

(C) *Civilization in the Middle East*

(D) *Muslim Science*

(E) *Culture and Language*

2. Which of the following is *not* used by the author in the presentation of his arguments?

    (A) Colonialism demoralized the local inhabitants.
    (B) Colonialism produced an identity crisis.
    (C) Cultural nationalism will soon disappear.
    (D) Decolonization does not always run smoothly.
    (E) Colonialists assumed that local cultures were inferior.

3. The author's attitude toward colonialism is best described as one of

    (A) sympathy   (D) hostility
    (B) bewilderment   (E) ambivalence
    (C) support

ANSWERS AND ANALYSIS

1. **(B)** Clearly, the main subject of the passage is nationalism. This is given in the statement on line 1, "Above all, colonialism was hated..." and in lines 29–31 and 38–39.

2. **(C)** Choice (E) is given in lines 1–2, (D) in lines 55–57, (B) in lines 31–33, and (A) is implied throughout; while the opposite of (C) is found in lines 42–44.

3. **(D)** See, for instance, the reference to "cultural racism" in lines 23–24, as well as the general tone of paragraph 1.

READING COMPREHENSION STRATEGIES

1. Use only the information in the passage.
2. Read the questions first, then the passage.
3. Note key words and ideas on your scratch paper.
4. Read *all* the answer alternatives.
5. Learn to identify the major question types.

3

SENTENCE CORRECTION REVIEW

DESCRIPTION OF THE TEST

The Sentence Correction questions test your understanding of the basic rules of English grammar and usage. To succeed on these questions, you need a command of sentence structure including tense and mood, subject and verb agreement, proper case, parallel structure, and other basics. No attempt is made to test for punctuation, spelling, or capitalization.

You will be given a sentence in which all or part of the sentence is underlined. You will then be asked to choose the best phrasing of the underlined part from five alternatives. (A) will always be the original phrasing.

TEST-TAKING TIPS

1. Read the sentence, concentrating on the underlined part.
2. Check for pronoun errors. (Look for errors in words like *he, him, her, we, us, them, who, whom, whoever, whomever, you, it, which,* or *that.*)
3. If there are no pronoun errors, check the verbs.
4. If you find no errors in either verbs or pronouns, look at adjectives and adverbs.
5. Other possible errors include the use of incorrect idioms and faulty parallelism.
6. If the sentence is correct, select (A) as your answer.

SAMPLE QUESTION WITH ANSWER AND ANALYSIS

Since the advent of cable television, at the beginning of <u>this decade, the video industry took</u> a giant stride forward in this country.

(A) this decade, the video industry took
(B) this decade, the video industry had taken
(C) this decade, the video industry has taken
(D) this decade saw the video industry taking
(E) the decade that let the video industry take

Answer:

(C)

Analysis:

The phrase "Since the advent..." demands a verb in the present perfect form; thus, "*has taken*," not "*took*," is correct. Choice (E) changes the meaning of the original sentence.

REVIEW OF ERRORS COMMONLY FOUND IN THE SENTENCE CORRECTION SECTION

Since you need only *recognize* errors in grammar and usage for this part of the exam, this section of the book will review those errors most commonly presented in the GMAT and teach you *what to look for*. We will not review the basic rules of grammar, such as the formation and use of the different tenses and the passive voice, the subjective and objective cases of pronouns, the position of adjectives and adverbs, and the like. We assume that a candidate for the GMAT is familiar with basic grammar, and we will concentrate on error recognition based on that knowledge.

VERB ERRORS

1. ERRORS IN VERB TENSE

Check if the correct verb *tense* has been used in the sentence.

INCORRECT: When I came home, the children still didn't finish dinner.

CORRECT: When I came home, the children still <u>hadn't finished</u> dinner.

In REPORTED SPEECH, check that the rule of *sequence of tenses* has been observed.

INCORRECT: She promised she will come.

CORRECT: She promised she <u>would</u> come.

2. ERRORS IN TENSE FORMATION

Check if the tense has been formed correctly. *Know* the past participle of irregular verbs!

INCORRECT: He throwed it out the window.

CORRECT: He <u>threw</u> it out the window.

3. ERRORS IN SUBJECT-VERB AGREEMENT

Check if the subject of the verb is singular or plural. Does the verb agree in number?

Multiple subjects will be connected by the word AND:

Ted, John, <u>and</u> I <u>are</u> going.

If a singular subject is separated by a comma from an accompanying phrase, *it remains singular.*

<u>The bride</u>, together with the groom and her parents, <u>is receiving</u> at the door.

INCORRECT: There is many reasons why I can't help you.

CORRECT: There <u>are many reasons</u> why I can't help you.

4. ERRORS IN CONDITIONAL SENTENCES

In conditional sentences, the word *if* will NEVER be followed by the words *will* or *would.*

Here are the correct conditional forms:

FUTURE: If I <u>have</u> time, I <u>will do</u> it tomorrow.

PRESENT: If I <u>had</u> time, I <u>would do</u> it now.

PAST: If I <u>had had</u> time, I <u>would have done</u> it yesterday.

Sentences using the words *when, as soon as, the moment,* etc., are formed like future conditionals:

> I will tell him <u>if</u> I <u>see</u> him.
> I will tell him <u>when</u> I <u>see</u> him.

The verb *to be* will ALWAYS appear as *were* in the present conditional:

> If I <u>were</u> you, I wouldn't do that.
> She wouldn't say so if she <u>weren't</u> sure.

NOTE: Not all sentences containing *if* are conditionals. When *if* appears in the meaning of *whether,* it may take the future:

> I don't know <u>if</u> he <u>will be</u> there. (I don't know <u>whether</u> he will be there.)

INCORRECT: If I would have known, I wouldn't have gone.
CORRECT: If I <u>had known,</u> I wouldn't have gone.

5. ERRORS IN EXPRESSIONS OF DESIRE

Unfulfilled desires are expressed by the form "_____ had hoped that _____ would (or *could,* or *might*) do _____ ."

> I <u>had hoped</u> that I <u>would pass</u> the exam.
> Expressions with *wish* are formed as follows:

PRESENT: I wish I <u>knew</u> him.
FUTURE: I wish you <u>could</u> (<u>would</u>) <u>come</u>.
PAST: I wish he <u>had come</u> (or <u>could have come,</u> <u>would have come,</u> <u>might have come</u>).

NOTE: As in conditionals, the verb *to be* will ALWAYS appear as *were* in the present: I wish she <u>were</u> here.

INCORRECT: I wish I heard that story about him before I met him.
CORRECT: I wish I <u>had heard</u> (or <u>could have heard</u> or <u>would have heard</u>) that story about him before I met him.

6. ERRORS IN VERBS FOLLOWED BY VERB WORDS

The following list consists of words and expressions that are followed by a VERB WORD (the infinitive without the *to*):

ask	prefer	requirement
demand	recommend	suggest
desire	recommendation	suggestion
insist	require	urge

It is essential/imperative/important/necessary that…

INCORRECT: She ignored the doctor's recommendation that she stops smoking.

CORRECT: She ignored the doctor's recommendation that she <u>stop</u> smoking.

7. ERRORS IN NEGATIVE IMPERATIVES

Note the two forms for negative imperatives:

  a. Please <u>don't do</u> that.
  b. Would you please <u>not do</u> that.

INCORRECT: Would you please don't smoke here.
CORRECT: Please <u>don't smoke</u> here.
                    OR
  Would you please <u>not smoke</u> here.

8. ERRORS IN AFFIRMATIVE AND NEGATIVE AGREEMENT OF VERBS

Note the two correct forms for *affirmative* agreement:

  a. <u>I am</u> an American and <u>so is she</u>.
  b. <u>I am</u> an American and <u>she is too</u>.

  a. <u>Mary likes</u> Bach and <u>so does John</u>.
  b. <u>Mary likes</u> Bach and <u>John does too</u>.

  a. <u>My father will be</u> there and <u>so will my mother</u>.
  b. <u>My father will be</u> there and <u>my mother will too</u>.

INCORRECT: I have seen the film and she also has.
CORRECT: <u>I have seen</u> the film and <u>so has she</u>.

OR

<u>I have seen</u> the film and <u>she has too</u>.

Note the two correct forms for *negative* agreement:

    a. I'm not American and <u>he isn't either</u>.
    b. I'm not American and <u>neither is he</u>.

    a. Mary doesn't like Bach and <u>John doesn't either</u>.
    b. Mary doesn't like Bach and <u>neither does John</u>.

    a. My father won't be there and <u>my mother won't either</u>.
    b. My father won't be there and <u>neither will my mother</u>.

INCORRECT: I haven't seen the film and she hasn't neither.
CORRECT: I haven't seen the film and <u>she hasn't either</u>.

OR

I haven't seen the film and <u>neither has she</u>.

9. ERRORS OF INFINITIVES OR GERUNDS IN THE COMPLEMENT OF VERBS

Some verbs may be followed by either an infinitive or a gerund:

    I love <u>swimming</u> at night.
    I love <u>to swim</u> at night.

Other verbs, however, may require either one *or* the other for idiomatic reasons. Following is a list of the more commonly used verbs in this category:

Verbs requiring an INFINITIVE:

agree	fail	intend	promise
decide	hope	learn	refuse
expect	want	plan	

Verbs requiring a GERUND:

admit	deny	quit
appreciate	enjoy	regret
avoid	finish	risk
consider	practice	stop

Phrases requiring a GERUND:

approve of	do not mind	keep on
be better off	forget about	look forward to
can't help	insist on	think about
count on	get through	think of

INCORRECT: I intend learning French next semester.

CORRECT: I intend <u>to learn</u> French next semester.

10. ERRORS IN VERBS REQUIRING *HOW* IN THE COMPLEMENT

The verbs KNOW, TEACH, LEARN, and SHOW require the word *HOW* before an infinitive in the complement.

INCORRECT: She knows to drive.

CORRECT: She knows <u>how</u> to drive.

11. ERRORS IN TAG ENDINGS

Check for *three* things in tag endings:

- a. Does the ending use the *same person* as the sentence verb?
- b. Does the ending use the *same tense* as the sentence verb?
- c. If the sentence verb is positive, is the ending negative; if the sentence verb is negative, is the ending positive?

<u>It's</u> nice here, <u>isn't it</u>?
<u>It isn't</u> nice here, <u>is it</u>?

<u>She speaks</u> French, <u>doesn't she</u>?
<u>She doesn't speak</u> French, <u>does she</u>?

<u>They'll be</u> here tomorrow, <u>won't they</u>?
<u>They won't be</u> here tomorrow, <u>will they</u>?

EXCEPTIONS:

<u>I'm</u> right, <u>aren't I</u>?
<u>We ought</u> to go, <u>shouldn't we</u>?
<u>Let's</u> see, <u>shall we</u>?

NOTE: If there is a contraction in the sentence verb, make sure you know what the contraction stands for:

INCORRECT: She's been there before, isn't she?
CORRECT: She's been there before, hasn't she?

12. ERRORS IN IDIOMATIC VERB EXPRESSIONS

Following are a few commonly used idiomatic verb expressions. Notice whether they are followed by a verb word, a participle, an infinitive, or a gerund. Memorize a sample of each to check yourself when choosing an answer:

a. *must have (done)*—meaning "it is a logical conclusion"

They're late. They must have missed the bus.
There's no answer. They must have gone out.

b. *had better (do)*—meaning "it is advisable"

It's getting cold. You had better take your coat.
He still has a fever. He had better not go out yet.

c. *used to (do)*—meaning "was in the habit of doing in the past"

I used to smoke a pack of cigarettes a day, but I stopped.
When I worked on a farm, I used to get up at 4:30 in the morning.

d. *to be used to*—meaning "to be accustomed to"

to get used to
to become used to }—meaning "to become accustomed to"

The noise doesn't bother me; I'm used to studying with the radio on.
In America you'll get used to hearing only English all day long.

e. *make* someone *do*—meaning "force someone to do"
have someone *do*—meaning "cause someone to do"
let someone *do*—meaning "allow someone to do"

My mother made me take my little sister with me to the movies.

The teacher <u>had us write</u> an essay instead of taking an exam.
The usher didn't <u>let us come</u> in until the intermission.

f. *would rather*—meaning "would prefer"

I <u>would rather speak</u> to her myself.
I <u>would rather not speak</u> to her myself.

But if the preference is for someone *other than the subject* to do the action, use the PAST:

I <u>would rather</u> you <u>spoke</u> to her.
I <u>would rather</u> you <u>didn't speak</u> to her.

PRONOUN ERRORS

1. ERRORS IN PRONOUN SUBJECT/OBJECT

Check if a pronoun is the SUBJECT or the OBJECT of a verb or preposition.

INCORRECT: All of us—Fred, Jane, Alice, and me—were late.
CORRECT: <u>All of us</u>—Fred, Jane, Alice, and I—<u>were</u> late.

2. ERRORS WITH WHO AND WHOM

When in doubt about the correctness of WHO/WHOM, try substituting the subject/object of a simpler pronoun to clarify the meaning:

I don't know <u>who/whom</u> Sarah meant.

Try substituting *he/him;* then rearrange the clause in its proper order:

<u>he/him</u> Sarah meant/Sarah meant <u>him</u>.

Now it is clear that the pronoun is the *object* of the verb *meant*, so *whom* is called for.

CORRECT: I don't know <u>whom</u> Sarah meant.

ANOTHER EXAMPLE:
There was a discussion as to <u>who/whom</u> was better suited.

Try substituting *she/her*.

<u>she</u> was better suited/<u>her</u> was better suited.

Here the pronoun is the *subject* of the verb *was suited:*

CORRECT: There was a discussion as to <u>who</u> was better suited.

3. ERRORS OF PRONOUN SUBJECT-VERB AGREEMENT

Check if the pronoun and its verb agree in number. Remember that the following are *singular:*

anyone	either	neither	what
anything	everyone	no one	whatever
each	everything	nothing	whoever

These are *plural:*

both	many	several	others
few			

INCORRECT: John is absent, but a few of the class is here.

CORRECT: John is absent, but <u>a few</u> of the class <u>are</u> here.

INCORRECT: Everyone on the project have to come to the meeting.

CORRECT: <u>Everyone</u> on the project <u>has</u> to come to the meeting.

NOTE: In the forms *either ... or* and *neither ... nor*, the word directly preceding the verb will determine whether the verb should be singular or plural:

Either his parents or <u>he is</u> bringing it.
Either he or <u>his parents</u> <u>are</u> bringing it.

Neither his parents nor <u>he was</u> there.
Neither he nor <u>his parents</u> <u>were</u> there.

4. ERRORS OF POSSESSIVE PRONOUN AGREEMENT

Check if possessive pronouns agree in *person* and *number.*

INCORRECT: If anyone calls, take their name.

CORRECT: If <u>anyone</u> calls, take <u>his</u> name.

5. ERRORS IN PRONOUNS AFTER THE VERB TO BE

TO BE is an intransitive verb and will always be followed by a subject pronoun.

INCORRECT: It must have been her at the door.

CORRECT: It must have <u>been she</u> at the door.

6. ERRORS IN POSITION OF RELATIVE PRONOUNS

A relative pronoun refers to the word preceding it. If the meaning is unclear, the pronoun is in the wrong position.

INCORRECT: He could park right in front of the door, which was very convenient.

Since it was not the door which was convenient, the "which" is illogical in this position. In order to correct the sentence, it is necessary to rewrite it completely:

CORRECT: His being allowed to park right in front of the door was very convenient.

7. ERRORS IN PARALLELISM OF IMPERSONAL PRONOUNS

In forms using impersonal pronouns, use *either* "one ... one's/his or her" *or* "you ... your."

INCORRECT: One should take your duties seriously.

CORRECT: <u>One</u> should take <u>one's</u>/<u>his or her</u> duties seriously.

OR

<u>You</u> should take <u>your</u> duties seriously.

ADJECTIVE AND ADVERB ERRORS

1. ERRORS IN THE USE OF ADJECTIVES AND ADVERBS

Check if a word modifier is an ADJECTIVE or an ADVERB. Make sure the correct form has been used.

An ADJECTIVE describes a <u>noun</u> and answers the question *What kind?*

She is a <u>good</u> cook. (What kind of cook?)

An ADVERB describes either a <u>verb</u> or an <u>adjective</u> and answers the question *How?*

She cooks <u>well</u>. (She cooks how?)

This exercise is <u>relatively</u> <u>easy</u>. (How easy?)

Most adverbs are formed by adding *-ly* to the adjective.

EXCEPTIONS:

Adjective	Adverb
early	early
fast	fast
good	well
hard	hard *(hardly means almost not)*
late	late *(lately means recently)*

INCORRECT: I sure wish I were rich!

CORRECT: I <u>surely</u> wish I were rich!

2. ERRORS OF ADJECTIVES WITH VERBS OF SENSE

The following verbs of sense are intransitive and are described by ADJECTIVES:

be	look	smell	taste
feel	seem	sound	

INCORRECT: She looked very well.

CORRECT: She looked very <u>good</u>.

NOTE: "He is well" is also correct in the meaning of "He is healthy" or in describing a person's well-being.

INCORRECT: The food tastes deliciously.

CORRECT: The food tastes <u>delicious</u>.

NOTE: When the above verbs are used as transitive verbs, modify with an adverb, as usual: She tasted the soup <u>quickly</u>.

3. ERRORS IN COMPARATIVES

a. Similar comparison

ADJECTIVE: She is <u>as</u> <u>pretty</u> <u>as</u> her sister.

ADVERB: He works <u>as</u> <u>hard</u> <u>as</u> his father.

b. Comparative (of two things)

ADJECTIVE: She is <u>prettier than</u> her sister.

She is <u>more beautiful than</u> her sister.

She is <u>less successful than</u> her sister.

ADVERB: He works <u>harder than</u> his father.

He reads <u>more quickly than</u> I.

He drives <u>less carelessly than</u> he used to.

NOTE 1: A pronoun following *than* in a comparison will be the *subject pronoun:*

You are prettier than <u>she</u> (is).

You drive better than <u>he</u> (does).

NOTE 2: In using comparisons, <u>adjectives</u> of one syllable, or of two syllables ending in *-y,* add *-er:* smart, smarter; pretty, prettier. Other words of more than one syllable use *more:* interesting, more interesting. <u>Adverbs</u> of one syllable add *-er,* longer adverbs use *more:* fast, faster*;* quickly, more quickly.

NOTE 3: The word *different* is followed by *from:*

You are <u>different from</u> me.

c. Superlative (comparison of more than two things)

ADJECTIVE: She is <u>the prettiest</u> girl <u>in</u> her class.

He is <u>the most successful</u> of his brothers.

This one is <u>the least interesting of</u> the three.

ADVERB: He plays <u>the best</u> of all.

He speaks <u>the most interestingly</u>.

He spoke to them <u>the least patronizingly</u>.

EXCEPTIONAL FORMS:

good	better	best
bad	worse	worst
much/many	more	most
little	less	least

INCORRECT: This exercise is harder then the last one.
CORRECT: This exercise is harder <u>than</u> the last one.

4. ERRORS IN PARALLEL COMPARISONS

In parallel comparisons, check if the correct form has been used.

INCORRECT: The more you practice, you will get better.
CORRECT: <u>The more</u> you practice, <u>the better</u> you will get.

5. ERRORS OF ILLOGICAL COMPARATIVES

Check comparisons to make sure they *make sense*.

INCORRECT: Alaska is bigger than any state in the United States.
CORRECT: Alaska is bigger than any <u>other</u> state in the United States. (If Alaska were bigger than *any state*, it would be bigger than itself!)

6. ERRORS OF IDENTICAL COMPARISONS

Something can be *the same as* OR *like* something else. Do not mix up the two forms.

INCORRECT: Your dress is the same like mine.
CORRECT: Your dress is <u>like</u> mine.

OR

Your dress is <u>the same as</u> mine.

7. ERRORS IN IDIOMS USING COMPARATIVE STRUCTURES

Some idiomatic terms are formed like comparatives, although they are not true comparisons:

as high as	as much as	as few as
as little as	as many as	

INCORRECT: You may have to spend so much as two hours waiting.
CORRECT: You may have to spend <u>as much as</u> two hours waiting.

8. ERRORS IN NOUN-ADJECTIVES

When a NOUN is used as an ADJECTIVE, treat it as an adjective. Do not pluralize or add *s*.

INCORRECT: You're talking like a two-years-old child!

CORRECT: You're talking like a <u>two-year-old</u> child!

9. ERRORS IN ORDINAL AND CARDINAL NUMBERS

Ordinal numbers (first, second, third, etc.) are preceded by *the*. Cardinal numbers (one, two, three, etc.) are not.

We missed <u>the first</u> act.

We missed Act <u>One</u>.

NOTE: Ordinarily, either form is correct. There are two exceptions:

a. In *dates* use only *ordinal* numbers:

May <u>first</u> (*not* May one)

the <u>first</u> of May

b. In terms dealing with *travel*, use only *cardinal* numbers, as "Gate Three" may not actually be the third gate. It is <u>Gate Number Three</u>.

INCORRECT: We leave from the second pier.

CORRECT: We leave from Pier <u>Two</u>.

10. ERRORS IN MODIFYING COUNTABLE AND NONCOUNTABLE NOUNS

If a noun can be preceded by a number, it is a countable noun and will be modified by these words:

| a few | many, more | some |
| few, fewer | number of | |

If it cannot be preceded by a number, it is noncountable and will be modified by these words:

| amount of | little, less | some |
| a little | much, more | |

INCORRECT: I was surprised by the large amount of people who came.

CORRECT: I was surprised by the large <u>number of people</u> who came.

ERRORS IN USAGE

1. ERRORS IN CONNECTORS

There are several ways of connecting ideas. Do not mix the different forms:

and	also	not only…but also
too	as well as	both…and

INCORRECT: She speaks not only Spanish but French as well.

CORRECT: She speaks Spanish <u>and</u> French.

She speaks Spanish. She <u>also</u> speaks French.

She speaks Spanish <u>and</u> French <u>too</u>.

She speaks <u>not only</u> Spanish <u>but also</u> French.

She speaks <u>both</u> Spanish <u>and</u> French.

She speaks Spanish <u>as well as</u> French.

2. ERRORS IN QUESTION WORD CONNECTORS

When a question word such as *when* or *what* is used as a connector, the clause that follows is *not* a question. Do not use the interrogative form.

INCORRECT: Do you know when does the movie start?

CORRECT: Do you know <u>when</u> the movie <u>starts</u>?

3. ERRORS IN PURPOSE CONNECTORS

The word *so* by itself means *therefore*.

     It was too hot to study, <u>so</u> we went to the beach.

   So that means *in order to* or *in order that*.

INCORRECT: We took a cab so we would be on time.

CORRECT: We took a cab <u>so that</u> we would be on time.

4. ERRORS WITH BECAUSE

It is incorrect to say: *The reason is because…* Use: *The reason is that…*

INCORRECT: The reason he was rejected was because he was too young.

CORRECT: The reason he was rejected was <u>that</u> he was too young.

OR

He was rejected <u>because of</u> his young age.

OR

He was rejected <u>because</u> he was too young.

5. ERRORS OF DANGLING MODIFIERS

An introductory verbal modifier should be directly followed by the noun or pronoun that it modifies. Such a modifier will start with a gerund or participial phrase and be followed by a comma. Look for the modified noun or pronoun *immediately* after the comma.

INCORRECT: Seeing that the hour was late, it was decided to post-pone the committee vote.

CORRECT: <u>Seeing</u> that the hour was late, <u>the committee</u> decided to postpone the vote.

6. ERRORS IN PARALLEL CONSTRUCTION

In sentences containing a series of two or more items, check to see if the same form has been used for all the items in the series. Do *not* mix infinitives with gerunds, adjectives with participial phrases, or verbs with nouns.

INCORRECT: The film was interesting, exciting, and it was made well.

CORRECT: The film was <u>interesting</u>, <u>exciting</u>, and <u>well made</u>.

7. ERRORS OF UNNECESSARY MODIFIERS

In general, the more simply an idea is stated, the better it is. An adverb or adjective can often eliminate extraneous words.

INCORRECT: He drove in a careful way.

CORRECT: He drove carefully.

Beware of words with the same meaning in the same sentence.

INCORRECT: The new innovations were startling.

CORRECT: The innovations were startling.

Beware of general wordiness.

INCORRECT: That depends on the state of the general condition of the situation.

CORRECT: That depends on the situation.

8. ERRORS OF COMMONLY CONFUSED WORDS

Following are some of the more commonly misused words in English:

a. **to lie**	lied	lied	lying	to tell an untruth
to lie	lay	lain	lying	to recline
to lay	laid	laid	laying	to put down (*Idiomatic* usage: LAY THE TABLE, put dishes, etc., on the table; CHICKENS LAY EGGS; LAY A BET, make a bet)
b. **to rise**	rose	risen	rising	to go up; to get up
to arise	arose	arisen	arising	to wake up; to get up (*Idiomatic* usage: A PROBLEM HAS ARISEN, a problem has come up)
to raise	raised	raised	raising	to lift; bring up (*Idiomatic* usage: TO RAISE CHILDREN, to bring up children; TO RAISE VEGETABLES, to grow vegetables; TO RAISE MONEY, to collect funds for a cause)
c. **to set**	set	set	setting	to put down (*Idiomatic* usage: SET A DATE, arrange a date; SET THE TABLE, put dishes, etc., on the table; THE SUN SET, the sun went down

for the night; TO SET THE CLOCK, to adjust the timing mechanism of a clock)

to sit	sat	sat	sitting	to be in or get into a sitting position
d. **to let**	let	let	letting	to allow; to rent
to leave	left	left	leaving	to go away

e. **formerly**—previously
  formally—in a formal way

f. **to affect**—to influence (verb)
  effect—result (noun)

INCORRECT: He was laying in bed all day yesterday.
CORRECT: He was <u>lying</u> in bed all day yesterday.

INCORRECT: The price of gas has raised three times last year.
CORRECT: The price of gas <u>rose</u> three times last year.

OR

The price of gas <u>was raised</u> three times last year.

INCORRECT: He raised slowly from his chair.
CORRECT: He <u>arose</u> slowly from his chair.

9. ERRORS OF MISUSED WORDS AND PREPOSITIONAL IDIOMS

a. **in spite of; despite**

The two expressions are synonymous; use *either* one *or* the other.

INCORRECT: They came despite of the rain.
CORRECT: They came <u>in spite of</u> the rain.

OR

They came <u>despite</u> the rain.

b. **scarcely; barely; hardly**

All three words mean *almost not at all;* do NOT use a negative with them.

INCORRECT: I hardly never see him.
CORRECT: I <u>hardly ever</u> see him.

INCORRECT: He has scarcely no money.
CORRECT: He has <u>scarcely any</u> money.

   c. Note and memorize the prepositions in these common idioms:

approve/disapprove <u>of</u>	agree/disagree <u>with</u>
be ashamed <u>of</u>	compare <u>with</u> (point out
capable/incapable <u>of</u>	similarities between things of a
be conscious <u>of</u>	different order)
be afraid <u>of</u>	compare <u>to</u> (point out differences
independent <u>of</u>	between things of the same
in the habit <u>of</u>	order)
be interested <u>in</u>	be equal <u>to</u>
except <u>for</u>	next <u>to</u>
dependent <u>on</u>	related <u>to</u>
be bored <u>with</u>	similar <u>to</u>

A TACTIC FOR SENTENCE CORRECTION QUESTIONS

The first step in the Sentence Correction part of the exam is to read the sentence carefully in order to spot an error of grammar or usage. Once you have found an error, eliminate choice (A) and ALL OTHER ALTERNATIVES CONTAINING THAT ERROR. Concentrate on the remaining alternatives to choose your answer. Do not select an alternative that has changed the *meaning* of the original sentence.

EXAMPLE 1:

If I knew him better, <u>I would have insisted that he change</u> the hour of the lecture.

   (A) I would have insisted that he change
   (B) I would have insisted that he changed
   (C) I would insist that he change
   (D) I would insist for him to change
   (E) I would have insisted him to change

Since we must assume the unmarked part of the sentence to be correct, this is a PRESENT CONDITIONAL sentence; therefore, the second verb in the sentence should read *I would insist.* Glancing through the alternatives, you can eliminate (A), (B), and (E). You are left with (C) and (D). Remember that the word *insist* takes a *verb word* after it. (C) is the only correct answer.

If you do not find any grammatical error in the underlined part, read the alternatives to see if one of them uses a clearer or more concise style to express the same thing. Do not choose an alternative that changes the meaning of the original sentence.

EXAMPLE 2:
The couple, who had been married recently, booked their honeymoon passage through an agent who lived near them.

(A) The couple, who had been married recently, booked their honeymoon passage through an agent who lived near them.
(B) The couple, who had been recently married, booked their honeymoon passage through an agent who lived not far from them.
(C) The newlyweds booked their honeymoon passage through a local agent.
(D) The newlyweds booked their passage through an agent that lived not far from them.
(E) The couple lived not far from the agent who through him they booked their passage.

Although (A), the original, has no real errors, (C) expresses the same thing more concisely, without distorting the original meaning of the sentence.

Remember: If you find no errors, and if you find that none of the alternatives improve the original, choose (A).

PRACTICE EXERCISE WITH ANSWERS AND ANALYSIS

Directions: This exercise consists of a number of sentences, in each of which some part or the whole is underlined. Each sentence is followed by five alternative versions of the underlined portion. Select the alternative you consider both most correct and most effective according to the requirements of standard written English. Answer (A) is the same as the original version; if you think the original version is best, select answer (A).

In considering the answer choices, be attentive to matters of grammar, diction, and syntax, as well as clarity, precision, and fluency. Do not select an answer that alters the meaning of the original sentence.

1. A good doctor inquires not only about patients' physical health, <u>but about their mental health too</u>.

    (A) but about their mental health too

    (B) but their mental health also

    (C) but also inquires about their mental health

    (D) but also about their mental health

    (E) but too about their mental health

2. <u>Knowing that the area was prone to earthquakes</u>, all the buildings were reinforced with additional steel and concrete.

    (A) Knowing that the area was prone to earthquakes,

    (B) Having known that the area was prone to earthquakes,

    (C) Since the area was known to be prone to earthquakes,

    (D) Since they knew that the area was prone to earthquakes,

    (E) Being prone to earthquakes,

3. John would never have taken the job <u>if he had known</u> what great demands it would make on his time.

    (A) if he had known

    (B) if he knew

    (C) if he had been knowing

    (D) if he knows

    (E) if he was knowing

ANSWERS AND ANALYSIS

1. **(D)** The connective *not only* MUST be accompanied by *but also*. Eliminate (A), (B), and (E). (C) repeats *inquires* unnecessarily. (D) is correct.

2. **(C)** *All the buildings* couldn't have known that the area was prone to earthquakes. Since the unmarked part of the sentence must be assumed to be correct, eliminate all alternatives beginning with a dangling modifier: (A), (B), and (E). In (D) the word *they* is unclear. Where there is no definite subject, the passive is preferable. (C) is correct.

3. **(A)** This is a past conditional sentence. (A) is correct.

SENTENCE CORRECTION STRATEGIES

1. Remember that any error in the sentence must be in the underlined part.

2. If you determine that there is an error in the underlined part of the sentence, immediately eliminate answer choice (A).

3. Do not choose as an answer any alternative that changes the meaning of the original sentence.

4. Determine if the parts of the sentence are linked logically.

5. Look at the changes made in the answer alternatives.

6. Be aware of the common grammar and usage errors tested on the GMAT.

4

CRITICAL REASONING REVIEW

DESCRIPTION OF THE TEST

The Critical Reasoning questions are designed to test your ability to evaluate an assumption, inference, or argument. Each question consists of a short statement followed by a question or assumption about the statement. Each question or assumption has five possible answers. Your task is to evaluate each of the five possible choices and select the one that is the best alternative.

TEST-TAKING TIPS

1. *Before reading the passage, read the questions pertaining to it.* By reading the questions first, *carefully,* you familiarize yourself with the type of argument being presented and the factors you will have to consider in choosing your answer.

2. *Look for the conclusion first.* Critical reasoning questions are preceded by an argument or statement that has a conclusion or claim. While it may seem logical that a conclusion appears at the end of a passage, it might be given at the beginning or in the middle.

3. *Find the premises.* Premises are facts or evidence. Determine whether the conclusion follows logically from the premises or whether it is merely alleged. A conclusion may not follow, even though premises may be true. You must determine the legitimacy of assumptions and final conclusions.

TYPES OF QUESTIONS

Inference or Assumption. These questions test your ability to evaluate an assumption, inference, or argument. You will be given a statement, position, argument, or fact and will be asked to identify a conclusion or claim and the premise on which it is based.

Flaws. In this type of question you are asked to choose the best alternative answer that either represents a flaw in the statement position, or, if true, would weaken the argument or conclusion.

Statements of Fact. With this type of question, you will be asked to find the answer that best agrees with, summarizes, or completes the statement.

IDENTIFYING THE PREMISE AND CONCLUSION

In evaluating an argument and its strength and validity, the first step is to identify the components—the premises and conclusion. There are several things to keep in mind when doing this.

Cue Words. Very often you will be helped in identifying the parts of an argument by the presence of cue words. Words such as "if," "given that," "since," "because," "for," "suppose," and "in view of" signal the presentation of evidence and reasons in support of a fact or claim. These cues identify premises. Conclusions, on the other hand, may often be preceded by words such as "thus," "hence," "so," and "therefore." Without cue words, identifying and analyzing an argument becomes more difficult.

Position of Conclusion. Conclusions do not have to be at the end of an argument. Conclusions and premises may be reversed while the same meaning is conveyed. For example:

> "David was talking during the lesson, so he didn't understand the teacher's instructions."

> "David did not understand the teacher's instructions because he was talking during the lesson."

In both statements, the conclusion is "David did not understand the teacher's instructions."

Connecting Events to Draw Conclusions. Arguments frequently contain a number of premises and possibly more than one conclusion. Therefore, it is necessary to classify and connect things and events in order to analyze the arguments. To aid this analysis, think of events in terms of time sequence or causal relationships. For example:

> "Sarah overslept, which caused her to be late leaving for school; therefore, she ran all the way, causing her to be out of breath."

Determining What the Writer Is Trying to Prove. At first glance the analysis of some arguments looks difficult because of the absence of cue words. In these cases, ask yourself, "What is the writer trying to prove?" Once you have identified the main point of the argument, define it. Ask "How great a claim (or 'How limited a claim') is the author making?" "What precisely is the author talking about?" "What was the author's purpose in making the claim?"

To answer the first of these questions, look again for signal words—for instance "all," "none," "never," "always," "some," and "sometimes." There is a big difference, for example, between "all cars are red" and "some cars are red." The first statement is false. The second is most definitely true. Similarly, note the difference between "I have never seen him before" and "I have not seen him today."

Often the use of different verbs and adverbs can change the meaning of similar claims. "The ground was wet, so it must have been raining." We can limit the claim by changing "must" to "probably." "The ground was wet. So it probably has been raining." The first statement stands more chance of being proven false. Anything else that can be shown to have made the ground wet limits the chance that it must have been the rain that caused the wetness. However, it could still have been raining, and there is always the probability, no matter how small, that it may have been.

Descriptive words, both nouns and adjectives, in a passage are also used to limit or expand claims made by another. Take the example:

"Prisoners in San Quentin rioted today because they were angry about their conditions."

The author's choice of the word "Prisoners" indicates merely that more than one prisoner rioted. Maybe all or maybe only some prisoners rioted. Note also that the author claims to know the reason for the riot—namely, that the prisoners were angry about their conditions and for no other reason. However, you cannot assume that just because an author states a reason for a claim, he or she is correct in that assumption. And if an author makes a claim about the cause of some event, he or she may either endorse or condemn it. Endorsement of a claim without any supporting evidence is not a substitute for proof.

The use of assumptions is vital in evaluating an argument, but the strength of an argument depends on the legitimacy of its assumptions.

DEDUCTIVE AND INDUCTIVE ARGUMENTS

An argument may be deductive or inductive, depending on how the conclusion follows or is inferred from the premises.

An argument may be defined as deductive if it is *impossible* for the conclusion to be false if all the premises are true. In other words, in a deductive argument, the premises necessitate the conclusion. An example of a deductive argument is:

(1) All men are mortal.
(2) Brian is a man.
(3) Therefore, Brian is a mortal.

If both premises are true, then the conclusion follows automatically.

An argument is inductive if it is *improbable* that the conclusion is false if all premises are true. The premises do not necessitate but do make probable the conclusion. The conclusion may be false even if all the premises are true.

Determining if the conclusion in an argument has been arrived at through deductive reasoning or through inductive reasoning can often be discerned from the wording of the statement or sentence.

Words such as "usually," "sometimes," and "generally" are usually signals of induction.

An example of an inductive argument is:

(1) Freshmen usually find economics I difficult.
(2) Jones is a freshman.
(3) Therefore, Jones finds economics I difficult.

In the above statement, both premises are true. If the premises are true, does the conclusion automatically follow? No, because not all freshmen find economics I difficult, and Jones may be one of the minority of freshmen who do not.

The distinction between deduction and induction should not be taken as a distinction between a good or superior way of arguing or reasoning and an inferior way. An inductive argument is not necessarily a bad argument. The two methods of argument serve different and complementary purposes. The distinction is in the manner by which a conclusion follows its premise(s).

DETERMINING THE LOGICAL SEQUENCE OF AN ARGUMENT

Having discussed types of arguments, we will now demonstrate in more detail how an argument can be identified and analyzed. You must be able to determine what the writer is trying to establish.

In order to identify an argument:

1. Find the conclusion first. This may be done by locating the cue that introduces the conclusion.
2. Find the premise(s). Again, locate the cue words (if present) that signal premises.
3. Determine if the premise(s) are true.
4. Determine the logical form of the argument.

ATTACKING THE ASSUMPTIONS OF AN ARGUMENT

In the GMAT, one often has to attack or find a fact that weakens an argument. The most effective way of doing this is to defeat the assumptions. Consider the following argument:

(1) Cooking classes take place on Tuesdays.

(2) Today is Tuesday.

(3) Therefore, cooking classes take place today.

We may be able to defeat this argument by analyzing the first premise. If we assume that cooking classes usually take place on a Tuesday, then there is a probability that if today is Tuesday it will be one of those Tuesdays when cooking classes are held, but this is obviously not certain. Premise (1) does not state that cooking classes take place every Tuesday; classes could be held every other Tuesday or every third Tuesday. Therefore, the third sentence, the conclusion of the argument, *may* be false.

Often, the attack on the argument will not be so obvious because the assumptions on which the argument is built are hidden or concealed. Someone who is making a totally honest and correct argument will not explicitly acknowledge all of the assumptions he or she makes. These hidden assumptions may be open to attack. Bear this in mind, particularly if you are presented with an argument that seems logical and correct but which reaches a factually impossible or absurd result. This could indicate the existence of hidden assumptions that make the argument invalid.

FALLACIES

As mentioned earlier, the thought process that links the premise of an argument to its conclusion is called an inference. Errors may occur in any part of the argumentation process. These errors in reasoning are called *fallacies*, or *flaws*.

A fallacy is a form of reasoning that is illogical or violates the rules of argumentation. A fallacy is, in other words, an argument that seems to be sound but is not. The following common types of fallacies are those that appear most often on the GMAT.

GUILT BY ASSOCIATION

One type of fallacy is guilt by association. Suppose that one proves that educator John Doe is a dues-paying member of the

Association for Fairy Teeth (A.F.T.), a fact not denied by Doe. Suppose that three members of the association have been found to be subversives. An argument may be:

> (1) John Doe is a member of the A.F.T.
> (2) X, Y, and Z are members of the A.F.T. and subversives.
> (3) Therefore, John Doe is a subversive.

This argument involves an invalid induction from premise (2) to a (missing) premise: all members of the A.F.T. are subversives. This has not been proven in the argument. It is left for the reader to draw his or her own—in this case, fallacious—conclusion, namely, that John Doe is a subversive.

FAULTY ANALOGY

Another type of fallacy is that of faulty analogy. A faulty analogy assumes that things that are similar in one respect must be similar in other respects. In general, analogies may be a useful form of communication. They enable a speaker to convey concepts in terms already familiar to the audience. A statement such as "our civilization is flowering" may be helpful in making a point, but the generalization is faulty. May we conclude that civilizations are in need of fertilizer?

Suppose that an economist argues that a "tariff on textiles will help our textile industry; a tariff on steel will help the steel industry; a tariff on every imported product will benefit the economy."

The above analogy may be stated as:

> (1) Tariffs on textiles benefit the textile industry.
> (2) Tariffs on steel benefit the steel industry.
> (3) Therefore, a tariff on every imported product benefits the economy.

The analogy here assumes that, because two industries benefit from tariffs, all others will also benefit. However, no proof for this argument is given.

CAUSAL FALLACIES

Some of the common causal fallacies are treating an insignificant relationship as a causal factor and assuming that a sequential relationship implies a causal relationship. That two events occur in sequence is not evidence of a causal relationship. For example, Herbert Hoover was elected President of the United States in 1928, an act followed by a recession in 1929. Did Hoover's policies cause the recession or were there other intervening factors? (There were.)

FALLACIES OF RELEVANCE

Fallacies of relevance involve arguments wherein one or more of the premises are irrelevant to the conclusion. For example:

Ad Hominem (Personal attacks). One type of fallacy of relevance is the *ad hominem* fallacy. In this type of fallacy, the person is attacked, not his or her argument. Attacking an opponent may well be easier than rebutting the merit of the argument. The role of the demagogue is to assassinate the character of his or her opponent, thereby casting doubt on his/her argument.

For example, an economics professor exclaims to her class: "Even a freshman knows that good economists don't necessarily have to be good mathematicians." Or "Congressman Goodboy has argued eloquently in favor of increasing public spending in his district. Isn't he the same congressman who was accused of wasting taxpayers' money on new autobuses whose air conditioning systems didn't work?"

The fallacy in these examples is that arguments are not treated on their merit. The arguments follow the form:

(1) Z asserts B.

(2) Z would benefit if we accept B.

(3) Z's assertion of B is insufficient to accept B as true.

This sort of argument attempts to show that B is not a reliable source because of some self-interest.

FALLACIES OF LANGUAGE (AMBIGUITY)

Ambiguity occurs when there are two or more meanings for a word, phrase, statement, or expression, especially when the meanings are easily confused. Another problem occurs when it is not clear in what context the meaning is being used. Words and expressions such as "democracy," "teamwork," "the American way," and "payoff" have different meanings to different people and may be used in different contexts. For example, is the United States government a democracy in the same sense as the Indian government? Does teamwork mean the same thing to Japanese and American workers? The only way to avoid ambiguity is to carefully define the meaning of words in context.

Let us look at some cases where ambiguity is used with intent to deceive or confuse.

Equivocation (Double meaning). The fallacy of equivocation occurs when words or phrases that have more than one meaning are used. An arguer using this fallacy relies on the fact that the audience fails to realize that some word or expression occurring more than once is used in different ways. The ambiguity may occur in both premises or in a premise and the conclusion. In the following, for example, the structure of the argument is valid but an equivocation occurs.

(1) Happiness is the end of life (X is Y).
(2) The end of life is death (Y is Z).
(3) So happiness is death (X is Z).

The fallacy is that the expression "end of life" has a different meaning in each premise. What has been asserted with one sense of the expression is then wrongly regarded as having been proved with respect to the other expression. An equivocation has been committed on the expression.

Amphiboly (Double talk). This fallacy results whenever there is ambiguity in sentence structure. For example:

"Can you spell backwards?"

"I have filled out the claim form for my damaged car which I enclose."

FINAL HINTS

Sherlock Holmes once said, "When you have ruled out the possible solutions, only the impossible remain." Can this statement be a true guide to critical reasoning problems? When taking the test, be sure to relate the possible answers to the actual statements, without drawing on prior conceptions or possibly misconceptions. Each of us perceives a thing in his or her own way, but critical reasoning problems can only have one solution.

1. Never rule out the blatantly obvious; it may just be the only solution possible.
2. Never rule out the blatantly ridiculous; it could also be the only reasonable conclusion to be drawn from a specific set of criteria.
3. Always treat each conclusion in isolation, since only one answer can be correct.

CRITICAL REASONING STRATEGIES

1. **First, read the question, and then read the passage.**
2. **Learn to spot major critical reasoning question types.**
3. **Look for the conclusion first.**
4. **Find the premises.**
5. **Do not be opinionated.**
6. **Do not be overwhelmed by unfamiliar subjects.**

5

PROBLEM SOLVING AND DATA SUFFICIENCY REVIEW

PROBLEM SOLVING

DESCRIPTION OF THE TEST

The Quantitative section of the GMAT is designed to test your ability to work with numbers. There are a variety of questions in this section dealing with the basic principles of arithmetic, algebra, and geometry. These questions may take the form of word problems or require straight calculation. In addition, questions involving the interpretation of tables and graphs may be included.

The typical Problem Solving and Data Sufficiency section on the GMAT CAT consists of 37 questions that must be answered within a time limit of 75 minutes. These questions range from very easy to quite challenging and are not always arranged in order of difficulty. Make sure you budget your time so that you can try each question.

TEST-TAKING TIPS

1. If a problem involves geometry and a diagram is not provided, draw a picture.
2. Before you start to work a problem, check the answers to see how accurate the answer must be. For example, if all the answers are given in tenths, don't use five decimal places in your computations.
3. Don't waste time on unnecessary calculations. If you can answer the question by estimating or doing a rough

calculation, the time you save can be used to work on other questions. Keep this in mind especially when doing problems that involve tables or graphs.

4. Make sure your answer is in the units asked for. Change all measurements to the same units before you do any calculations.

5. Reread the question to make sure you answered the question that was asked as opposed to the question you THOUGHT would be asked.

6. If possible check your answer. For example, if you solve an equation, check that the number you obtained actually solves the equation. Always ask yourself if an answer makes sense.

7. You will not be allowed to use a calculator on the exam. Practice doing arithmetic without a calculator a week before the test.

8. Remember that you must answer all questions on the GMAT CAT. If you are unsure of the correct answer, eliminate one or more answers and make an educated guess. Be sure to budget your time so you can answer each question.

9. You cannot return to a question once you have confirmed your answer, so be satisfied that you have chosen the best answer before you move on.

10. Use the scratch paper for your calculations.

METHODS OF APPROACHING THE TEST

1. **Practice arithmetic.** Most problem solving sections contain one or two basic computational questions, such as multiplying two decimals or finding the largest number in a collection of fractions. *You cannot use a calculator on the GMAT,* so practice your arithmetic before you take the exam. You already know how to do basic computation; you just need to practice to improve your speed and accuracy.

2. **Try to think quantitatively.** If you want to improve your quantitative skills, you should exercise them frequently. When you go grocery shopping, try to figure out whether the giant size is cheaper per ounce than the economy size. When you look at the news, try to make comparisons when figures are given. If you get used to thinking quantitatively, the problem solving sections will be much easier and you will feel more confident about the entire exam.

SAMPLE PROBLEM SOLVING QUESTIONS WITH ANSWERS AND ANALYSIS

Time: 12 minutes

Solve the sample questions below, allowing yourself 12 minutes to complete all of them. As you work, try to make use of the above strategy. Any figure that appears with a problem is drawn as accurately as possible to provide information that may help in answering the question. All numbers used are real numbers.

1. A train travels from Albany to Syracuse, a distance of 120 miles, at the average rate of 50 miles per hour. The train then travels back to Albany from Syracuse. The total traveling time of the train is 5 hours and 24 minutes. What was the average rate of speed of the train on the return trip to Albany?

(A) 60 mph   (D) 40 mph
(B) 50 mph   (E) 35 mph
(C) 48 mph

2. A parking lot charges a flat rate of X dollars for any amount of time up to two hours, and $\frac{1}{6}X$ for each hour or fraction of an hour after the first two hours. How much does it cost to park for 5 hours and 15 minutes?

(A) $3X$ (D) $1\frac{1}{2}X$
(B) $2X$ (E) $1\frac{1}{6}X$
(C) $1\frac{2}{3}X$

Use the following table for questions 3–5.

NUMBER OF STUDENTS BY MAJOR IN STATE UNIVERSITY		
	1950	**1970**
Division of Business	990	2,504
Division of Sciences	350	790
Division of Humanities	1,210	4,056
Division of Engineering	820	1,600
Division of Agriculture	630	1,050
TOTAL	4,000	10,000

3. From 1950 to 1970, the change in the percentage of university students enrolled in Engineering was

(A) roughly no change
(B) an increase of more than 4%
(C) an increase of more than 1% but less than 4%
(D) a decrease of more than 4%
(E) a decrease of more than 1% but less than 4%

4. The number of students enrolled in Business in 1970 divided by the number of Business students in 1950 is

(A) almost 3
(B) about 2.5
(C) roughly 2
(D) about 1
(E) about 40%

5. By 1970 how many of the divisions had an enrollment greater than 200% of the enrollment of that division in 1950?

(A) 0   (D) 3
(B) 1   (E) 4
(C) 2

ANSWERS AND ANALYSIS

1. **(D)** The train took $120/50 = 2\frac{2}{5}$ hours to travel from Albany to Syracuse. Since the total traveling time of the train was $5\frac{2}{5}$ hours, it must have taken the train 3 hours for the trip from Syracuse to Albany. Since the distance traveled is 120 miles, the average rate of speed on the return trip to Albany was $(\frac{1}{3})$ (120) mph = 40 mph.

2. **(C)** It costs X for the first 2 hours. If you park 5 hours and 15 minutes there are 3 hours and 15 minutes left after the first 2 hours. Since this time is charged at the rate of $X/6$ for each hour or fraction thereof, it costs $4(X/6)$ for the last 3 hours and 15 minutes. Thus the total $X + \frac{4}{6}X = 1\frac{2}{3}X$.

3. **(D)** Since $820/4,000 = .205$, the percentage of university students enrolled in Engineering in 1950 was 20.5%; since $1,600/10,000 = .16$, the percentage in 1970 was 16%. Thus the percentage of university students enrolled in Engineering was 4.5% less in 1970 than it was in 1950.

4. **(B)** In 1950 there were 990 Business students and in 1970 there were 2,504. Since $(2.5) (1,000) = 2,500$, the correct answer is thus (B), about 2.5. Note that this is an easy way to save yourself time. Instead of dividing 990 into 2,504 to find the exact answer, simply use numbers close to the original numbers to get an estimate. In many cases this gives enough information to answer the question and saves valuable time.

5. **(D)** If a division in 1970 has more than 200% of the number of students it had in 1950, that means that the number of students more than doubled between 1950 and 1970. Therefore simply double each entry in the 1950 column and if this is less than the corresponding entry in the 1970 column, that division has more than 200% of the number of students it had in 1950. Since $(2)(990) = 1980$, which is less than 2,504, the number of Business students more

than doubled. Since $(2)(1,210) = 2,420$, which is less than 4,056, Humanities more than doubled, and because $(2)(350) = 700$, which is less than 790, Sciences more than doubled. Engineering did not double in size because $(2)(820) = 1640$, which is larger than 1,600. Also since $(2)(630) = 1,260$, which is larger than 1,050, the number of Agricultural students in 1970 was less than 200% of the number of Agricultural students in 1950. Therefore three of the divisions (Business, Humanities, and Sciences) more than doubled between 1950 and 1970.

PROBLEM SOLVING STRATEGIES

1. Don't waste time.

2. Don't perform unnecessary calculations.

3. Answer the question that is asked.

4. Use intelligent guessing to improve your score.

5. Do calculations on your scratch paper.

6. Remember that you cannot go back to a question once you've confirmed the answer.

7. Check your work if you can.

8. If a problem involves units, keep track of the units. Make sure your answer has the correct units.

9. Use numerical values to check answers that involve formulas.

DATA SUFFICIENCY

DESCRIPTION OF THE TEST

These questions, included in the Quantitative section of the GMAT, are designed to test your reasoning ability. Like the Problem Solving questions, they require a basic knowledge of the principles of arithmetic, algebra, and geometry. Each Data Sufficiency question consists of a mathematical problem and two statements containing information relating to it. You must decide whether the problem can be solved by using information from: (A) the first statement alone, but not the second statement alone; (B) the second statement alone, but not the first statement alone; (C) both statements together, but neither alone; or (D) either of the statements alone. Choose (E) if the problem cannot be solved, even by using both statements together. As in the Problem Solving questions, time is of the utmost importance. Approaching Data Sufficiency problems properly will help you use this time wisely.

TEST-TAKING TIPS

1. *Don't waste time figuring out the exact answer.* Always keep in mind that you are never asked to supply an answer for the problem; you need only determine if there is sufficient data available to find the answer. Once you know whether or not it is possible to find the answer with the given information, you are through. If you spend too much time doing unnecessary work on one question, you may not be able to finish the entire section.
2. *Don't make extra assumptions.* In particular, don't make inferences based on the diagram supplied with some problems. You can't really tell if an angle is 90 degrees or 89 degrees by looking at a picture.
3. *Use the strategies described below to improve your score on these questions.*

METHODS OF APPROACHING THE TEST

Practice working data sufficiency questions. Most people have not had much experience with these types of questions. The more examples you work out the better you will perform on this section of the test. By the time you have finished the sample exams, you should feel confident about your ability to answer Data Sufficiency questions.

Eliminate choices with three questions. A systematic analysis can improve your score on Data Sufficiency sections. By answering three questions, you will always arrive at the correct choice. In addition, if you can answer any one of the three questions, you can eliminate at least one of the possible choices so that you can make an intelligent guess.

The three questions are:

I Is the first statement alone sufficient to solve the problem?
II Is the second statement alone sufficient to solve the problem?
III Are both statements together sufficient to solve the problem?

As a general rule try to answer the questions in the order I, II, III, since in many cases you will not have to answer all three to get the correct choice.

Here is how to use the three questions:

If the answer to I is YES, then the only possible choices are (A) or (D). Now, if the answer to II is YES, the choice must be (D), and if the answer to II is NO, the choice must be (A).

If the answer to I is NO then the only possible choices are (B), (C), or (E). Now, if the answer to II is YES, then the choice must be (B), and if the answer to II is NO, the only possible choices are (C) or (E).

So, finally, if the answer to III is YES, the choice is (C), and if the answer to III is NO, the choice is (E).

A good way to see this is to use a decision tree.

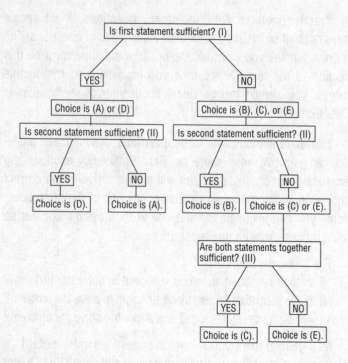

To use the tree simply start at the top and by answering YES or NO move down the tree until you arrive at the correct choice. For example, if the answer to I is YES and the answer to II is NO, then the correct choice is (A). (Notice that in this case you don't need to answer III to find the correct choice.)

The decision tree can also help you make intelligent guesses. If you can only answer one of the three questions, then you can eliminate the choices that follow from the wrong answer to the question.

Example 1.   You know the answer to I is YES. You can eliminate choices (B), (C), and (E).

Example 2.   You know the answer to II is NO. You can eliminate choices (D) and (B) since they follow from YES for II.

Example 3.   You know the answer to III is YES. You can eliminate choice (E) since it follows from NO for III.

Example 4.   You know the answer to I is NO and the answer to III is YES. You can eliminate (E) since it follows from NO to III. You also can eliminate (A) and (D) since they follow from YES to I.

Because you must answer every question, these guessing strategies can help you answer any data sufficiency question.

SAMPLE DATA SUFFICIENCY QUESTIONS WITH ANSWERS AND ANALYSIS

Time: 8 minutes

Directions: Each of the following problems has a question and two statements which are labeled (1) and (2). Use the data given in (1) and (2) together with other available information (such as the number of hours in a day, the definition of *clockwise,* mathematical facts, etc.) to decide whether the statements are *sufficient* to answer the question. Then choose

(A) if you can get the answer from (1) alone but not from (2) alone;

(B) if you can get the answer from (2) alone but not from (1) alone;

(C) if you can get the answer from (1) and (2) together, although neither statement by itself suffices;

(D) if statement (1) alone suffices and statement (2) alone suffices;

(E) if you cannot get the answer from statements (1) and (2) together, but need even more data.

All numbers used are real numbers. A figure given for a problem is intended to provide information consistent with that in the question, but not necessarily consistent with the additional information contained in the statements.

1. A rectangular field is 40 yards long. Find the area of the field.

   (1) A fence around the entire boundary of the field is 140 yards long.
   (2) The field is more than 20 yards wide.

2. Is X a number greater than zero?

   (1) $X^2 - 1 = 0$
   (2) $X^3 + 1 = 0$

3. An industrial plant produces bottles. In 2001 the number of bottles produced by the plant was twice the number produced in 2000. How many bottles were produced altogether in the years 2000, 2001, and 2002?

   (1) In 2002 the number of bottles produced was 3 times the number produced in 2000.
   (2) In 2003 the number of bottles produced was one half the total produced in the years 2000, 2001, and 2002.

4. A man 6 feet tall is standing near a light on the top of a pole. What is the length of the shadow cast by the man?

   (1) The pole is 18 feet high.
   (2) The man is 12 feet from the pole.

5. Find the length of RS if z is 90° and $PS = 6$.

   (1) $PR = 6$
   (2) $x = 45°$

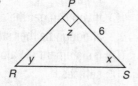

6. Working at a constant rate and by himself, it takes worker U 3 hours to fill up a ditch with sand. How long would it take for worker V to fill up the same ditch working by himself?

   (1) Working together but at the same time U and V can fill in the ditch in 1 hour 52½ minutes.
   (2) In any length of time worker V fills in only 60% as much as worker U does in the same time.

7. Did John go to the beach yesterday?

(1) If John goes to the beach, he will be sunburned the next day.

(2) John is sunburned today.

ANSWERS AND ANALYSIS

Answers:

1. **(A)**   4. **(C)**   7. **(E)**
2. **(B)**   5. **(D)**
3. **(E)**   6. **(D)**

Analysis:

1. **(A)** The area of a rectangle is the length multiplied by the width. Since you know the length is 40 yards, you must find out the width in order to solve the problem. Since statement (2) simply says the width is greater than 20 yards you cannot find out the exact width using (2). So (2) alone is not sufficient. Statement (1) says the length of a fence around the entire boundary of the field is 140 yards. The length of this fence is the perimeter of the rectangle, the sum of twice the length and twice the width. If we replace the length by 40 in $P = 2L + 2W$ we have $140 = 2(40) + 2W$ and solving for W yields $2W = 60$, or $W = 30$ yards. Hence the area is $(40)(30) = 1200$ square yards. Thus (1) alone is sufficient but (2) alone is not.

2. **(B)** Statement (1) means $X^2 = 1$, but there are two possible solutions to this equation, $X = 1$, $X = -1$. Thus using (1) alone you cannot deduce whether X is positive or negative. Statement (2) means $X^3 = -1$, but there is only one possible (real) solution to this, $X = -1$. Thus X is not greater than zero, which answers the question. And (2) alone is sufficient.

3. **(E)** T, the total produced in the three years, is the sum of $P_0 + P_1 + P_2$, where P_0 is the number produced in 2000, P_1 the number produced in 2001, and P_2 the number produced in 2002. You are given that $P_1 = 2P_0$. Thus $T = P_0 + P_1 + P_2 =$

$P_0 + 2P_0 + P_2 = 3P_0 + P_2$. So we must find out P_0 and P_2 to answer the question. Statement (1) says $P_2 = 3P_0$; thus, by using (1), if we can find the value of P_0, we can find T. But (1) gives us no further information about P_0. Statement (2) says $\frac{1}{2}T$ equals the number produced in 2003, but it does not say what this number is. Since there are no relations given between production in 2003 and production in the individual years 2000, 2001, or 2002, you cannot use (2) to find out what P_0 is. Thus (1) and (2) together are not sufficient.

4. **(C)** Sometimes it may help to draw a picture. By proportions or by similar triangles the height of the pole, h, is to 6 feet as the length of shadow, s, + the distance to the pole, x, is to s. So $h/6 = (s + x)/s$. Thus $hs = 6s + 6x$ by cross-multiplication. Solving for s gives $hs - 6s = 6x$, or $s(h - 6) = 6x$ or finally we have $s = 6x/(h - 6)$. Statement (1) says $h = 18$; thus $s = 6x/12 = x/2$, but using (1) alone we cannot deduce the value of x. Thus (1) alone is not sufficient. Statement (2) says x equals 12; thus using (1) and (2) together we deduce $s = 6$, but using (2) alone all we can deduce is that $s = 72/(h - 6)$, which cannot be solved for s unless we know h. Thus using (1) and (2) together we can deduce the answer, but (1) alone is not sufficient, nor is (2) alone.

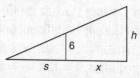

5. **(D)** Since z is a right angle, $(RS)^2 = (PS)^2 + (PR)^2$, so $(RS)^2 = (6)^2 + (PR)^2$, and RS will be the positive square root of $36 + (PR)^2$. Thus if you can find the length of PR the problem is solved. Statement (1) says $PR = 6$, thus $(RS)^2 = 36 + 36$, so $RS = 6\sqrt{2}$. Thus (1) alone is sufficient. Statement (2) says $x = 45°$ but, since the sum of the angles in a triangle is 180° and z is 90°, then $y = 45°$. So x and y are equal angles and that means the sides opposite x and opposite y must

be equal, or $PS = PR$. Thus $PR = 6$ and $RS = 6$, so (2) alone is also sufficient.

6. **(D)** (1) says U and V together can fill in the ditch in $1\frac{7}{8}$ hours. Since U can fill in the ditch in 3 hours, in 1 hour he can fill in one–third of the ditch. Hence, in $1\frac{7}{8}$ hours U would fill in $(\frac{1}{3})(\frac{15}{8}) = \frac{5}{8}$ of the ditch. So V fills in $\frac{3}{8}$ of the ditch in $1\frac{7}{8}$ hours. Thus V would take $(\frac{8}{3})(\frac{15}{8}) = 5$ hours to fill in the ditch working by himself. Therefore statement (1) alone is sufficient. According to statement (2), since U fills the ditch in 3 hours, V will fill $\frac{3}{5}$ of the ditch in 3 hours. Thus V will take 5 hours to fill in the ditch working by himself.

7. **(E)** Obviously, neither statement alone is sufficient. John *could* have gotten sunburned at the beach, but he might have gotten sunburned somewhere else. Therefore (1) and (2) together are not sufficient. This problem tests your grasp of an elementary rule of logic rather than your mathematical knowledge.

DATA SUFFICIENCY STRATEGIES

1. Make sure you understand the directions.
2. Don't waste time figuring out the exact answer.
3. Draw a picture whenever possible.
4. Don't make extra assumptions.
5. Use a system to work through the questions.

QUICK MATHEMATICS REVIEW

The Problem Solving and Data Sufficiency areas of the GMAT require a working knowledge of mathematical principles. The following is a brief review of topics that many people need to brush up on. If you want a more comprehensive review of mathematics, we recommend the review that appears in *Barron's GMAT, 15th Edition*.

ARITHMETIC

FRACTIONS

A *fraction* is a number which represents a ratio or division of two whole numbers (integers). A fraction is written in the form $\frac{a}{b}$. The number on the top, *a,* is called the numerator; the number on the bottom, *b,* is called the denominator. The denominator tells how many equal parts there are (for example, parts of a pie); the numerator tells how many of these equal parts are taken.

For example, $\frac{5}{8}$ is a fraction whose numerator is 5 and whose denominator is 8; it represents taking 5 of 8 equal parts, or dividing 8 into 5.

A fraction cannot have 0 as a denominator since division by 0 is not defined.

A fraction with 1 as the denominator is the same as the whole number which is its numerator. For example, $\frac{12}{1}$ is 12, $\frac{0}{1}$ is 0.

If the numerator and denominator of a fraction are identical, the fraction represents 1. For example, $\frac{3}{3} = \frac{9}{9} = \frac{13}{13} = 1$. Any whole number, *k,* is represented by a fraction with a numerator equal to *k* times the denominator. For example, $\frac{18}{6} = 3$, and $\frac{30}{5} = 6$.

Mixed Numbers

A *mixed number* consists of a whole number and a fraction. For example, $7\frac{1}{4}$ is a mixed number; it means $7 + \frac{1}{4}$ and $\frac{1}{4}$ is called the fractional part of the mixed number $7\frac{1}{4}$. Any mixed number can be changed into a fraction:

(A) Multiply the whole number by the denominator of the fractional part.

(B) Add the numerator of the fraction to the result of step A.

(C) Use the result of step B as the numerator and use the denominator of the fractional part of the mixed number as the denominator. This fraction is equal to the mixed number.

EXAMPLE:

Write $7\frac{1}{4}$ as a fraction.

(A) $4 \cdot 7 = 28$ (B) $28 + 1 = 29$ (C) so $7\frac{1}{4} = \frac{29}{4}$.

In calculations with mixed numbers, change the mixed numbers into fractions.

Multiplying Fractions

To multiply two fractions, multiply their numerators and divide this result by the product of their denominators.

In word problems, *of* usually indicates multiplication.

EXAMPLE:

John saves $\frac{1}{3}$ of $240. How much does he save?

$\frac{1}{3} \cdot \frac{240}{1} = \frac{240}{3} = \$80$, the amount John saves.

Dividing Fractions

One fraction is a *reciprocal* of another if their product is 1. So $\frac{1}{2}$ and 2 are reciprocals. To find the reciprocal of a fraction, simply interchange the numerator and denominator (turn the fraction upside down). This is called *inverting* the fraction. So when you invert $\frac{15}{17}$ you get $\frac{17}{15}$. When a fraction is inverted the inverted fraction and the original fraction are reciprocals. Thus $\frac{15}{17} \cdot \frac{17}{15} = \frac{255}{255} = \frac{1}{1} = 1$.

To divide one fraction (the dividend) by another fraction (the divisor), invert the divisor and multiply.

EXAMPLE:

$$\frac{5}{6} \div \frac{3}{4} = \frac{5}{6} \cdot \frac{4}{3} = \frac{20}{18}$$

Dividing and Multiplying by the Same Number

Since multiplication or division by 1 does not change the value of a number, you can multiply or divide any fraction by 1 and the fraction will remain the same. Remember that $\frac{a}{a} = 1$ for any nonzero number a. Therefore, if you multiply or divide any fraction by $\frac{a}{a}$, the result is the same as if you multiplied the numerator and denominator by a or divided the numerator and denominator by a.

If you multiply the numerator and denominator of a fraction by the same nonzero number, the fraction remains the same.

If you divide the numerator and denominator of any fraction by the same nonzero number, the fraction remains the same.

Consider the fraction $\frac{3}{4}$. If we multiply 3 by 10 and 4 by 10, then $\frac{30}{40}$ must equal $\frac{3}{4}$.

Equivalent Fractions

Two fractions are equivalent or equal if they represent the same ratio or number. In the last section, you saw that if you multiply or divide the numerator and denominator of a fraction by the same nonzero number the result is equivalent to the original fraction. For example,

$\frac{7}{8} = \frac{70}{80}$ since $70 = 10 \times 7$ and $80 = 10 \times 8$.

> *In the test, there will be only five choices, so the answer you come up with may not be the same as any of the given choices.* You may have to express a fraction as an equivalent fraction.

To find a fraction with a known denominator equal to a given fraction:

(A) divide the denominator of the given fraction into the known denominator;

(B) multiply the result of (A) by the numerator of the given fraction; this is the numerator of the required equivalent fraction.

EXAMPLE:

Find a fraction with a denominator of 30 which is equal to $\frac{2}{5}$:

(A) 5 into 30 is 6;

(B) $6 \cdot 2 = 12$ so $\frac{12}{30} = \frac{2}{5}$.

Reducing a Fraction to Lowest Terms

A fraction has been reduced to lowest terms when the numerator and denominator have no common factors. For example, $\frac{3}{4}$ is reduced to lowest terms, but $\frac{3}{6}$ is not because 3 is a common factor of 3 and 6.

> To reduce a fraction to lowest terms, cancel all the common factors of the numerator and denominator. (Cancelling common factors will not change the value of the fraction.)

For example, $\dfrac{100}{100} = \dfrac{10 \cdot 10}{10 \cdot 15} = \dfrac{10}{15} = \dfrac{5 \cdot 2}{5 \cdot 3} = \dfrac{2}{3}$. Since 2 and 3 have no common factors, $\dfrac{2}{3}$ is $\dfrac{100}{150}$ reduced to lowest terms. A fraction is equivalent to the fraction reduced to lowest terms.

Adding Fractions

If the fractions have the same denominator, then the denominator is called a *common denominator*. Add the numerators, and use this sum as the new numerator with the common denominator as the denominator of the sum.

If the fractions don't have the same denominator, you must first find a common denominator. Multiply all the denominators together; the result is a common denominator.

EXAMPLE:

To add $\dfrac{1}{2} + \dfrac{2}{3} + \dfrac{7}{4}$, multiply $2 \cdot 3 \cdot 4$ to get the common denominator (24).

There are many common denominators; the smallest one is called the *least common denominator*. For the previous example, 12 is the least common denominator.

Once you have found a common denominator, express each fraction as an equivalent fraction with the common denominator, and add as you did for the case when the fractions had the same denominator.

EXAMPLE:

$\dfrac{1}{2} + \dfrac{2}{3} + \dfrac{7}{4} = ?$

(A) 24 is a common denominator.

(B) $\dfrac{1}{2} = \dfrac{12}{24}, \dfrac{2}{3} = \dfrac{16}{24}, \dfrac{7}{4} = \dfrac{42}{24}$.

(C) $\dfrac{1}{2} + \dfrac{2}{3} + \dfrac{7}{4} = \dfrac{12}{24} + \dfrac{16}{24} + \dfrac{42}{24} = \dfrac{12+16+42}{24} = \dfrac{70}{24} = \dfrac{35}{12}$.

Subtracting Fractions

When the fractions have the same denominator, subtract the numerators and place the result over the denominator.

When the fractions have different denominators:

(A) Find a common denominator.
(B) Express the fractions as equivalent fractions with the same denominator.
(C) Subtract.

Complex Fractions

A fraction whose numerator and denominator are themselves fractions is called a *complex fraction*. For example, $\frac{\frac{2}{3}}{\frac{4}{5}}$ is a complex fraction. A complex fraction can always be simplified by dividing the fraction.

EXAMPLE:

$$\frac{2}{3} \div \frac{4}{5} = \frac{\overset{1}{\cancel{2}}}{3} \cdot \frac{5}{\underset{2}{\cancel{4}}} = \frac{1}{3} \cdot \frac{5}{2} = \frac{5}{6}$$

Converting a Fraction into a Decimal

To convert a fraction into a decimal, divide the denominator into the numerator. For example, $\frac{3}{4} = \frac{3.00}{4} = .75$. Some fractions give an infinite decimal when you divide the denominator into the numerator, for example, $\frac{1}{3} = .333\ldots$ where the three dots mean you keep on getting 3 with each step of division. $.333\ldots$ is an *infinite decimal*. If a fraction has an infinite decimal, use the fraction in any computation.

EXAMPLE:

What is $\frac{2}{9}$ of $3,690.90?

Since the decimal for $\frac{2}{9}$ is .2222…, use the fraction $\frac{2}{9}$.

$\frac{2}{9} \times \$3,690.90 = 2 \times \$410.10 = \$820.20.$

PERCENTAGE

Percentage is another method of expressing fractions or parts of an object. Percentages are expressed in terms of hundredths, so 100% means 100 hundredths or 1, and 50% would be 50 hundredths or $\frac{1}{2}$.

A decimal is converted to a percentage by multiplying the decimal by 100. Since multiplying a decimal by 100 is accomplished by moving the decimal point two places to the right, *you convert a decimal into a percentage by moving the decimal point two places to the right.* For example, .134 = 13.4%.

If you wish to convert a percentage into a decimal, you divide the percentage by 100. There is a shortcut for this also. To divide by 100 you move the decimal point two places to the left.

Therefore, *to convert a percentage into a decimal, move the decimal point two places to the left.* For example, 24% = .24.

A fraction is converted into a percentage by changing the fraction to a decimal and then changing the decimal to a percentage. A percentage is changed into a fraction by first converting the percentage into a decimal and then changing the decimal to a fraction.

When you compute with percentages, it is usually easier to change the percentages to decimals or fractions.

EXAMPLE 1:

A company has 6,435 bars of soap. If the company sells 20% of its bars of soap, how many bars of soap did it sell?

Change 20% into .2. Thus, the company sold (.2)(6,435) = 1287.0 = 1,287 bars of soap. An alternative method would be to convert 20% to $\frac{1}{5}$. Then $\frac{1}{5} \times 6,435 = 1,287$.

EXAMPLE 2:

If the population of Dryden was 10,000 in 1960 and the population of Dryden increased by 15% between 1960 and 1970, what was the population of Dryden in 1970?

The population increased by 15% between 1960 and 1970, so the increase was (.15)(10,000), which is 1,500. The population in 1970 was 10,000 + 1,500 = 11,500.

A quicker method: The population increased 15%, so the population in 1970 is 115% of the population in 1960. Therefore, the population in 1970 is 115% of 10,000, which is (1.15)(10,000) = 11,500.

INTEREST AND DISCOUNT

Two of the most common uses of percentages are in interest and discount problems.

The rate of interest is usually given as a percentage. The basic formula for interest problems is:

$$\text{INTEREST} = \text{AMOUNT} \times \text{TIME} \times \text{RATE}$$

You can assume the rate of interest is the annual rate of interest unless the problem states otherwise; so you should express the time in years.

EXAMPLE 1:

What annual rate of interest was paid if $5,000 earned $300 in interest in 2 years?

Since the interest was earned in 2 years, $150 is the interest earned in one year. $\dfrac{150}{5,000} = .03 = 3\%$, so the annual rate of interest was 3%.

This type of interest is called *simple interest*.

There is another method of computing interest called *compound interest*. In computing compound interest, the interest is periodically added to the amount (or principal) which is earning interest.

EXAMPLE 2:

What will $1,000 be worth after three years if it earns interest at the rate of 5% compounded annually?

Compounded annually means that the interest earned during one year is added to the amount (or principal) at the end of each year. The interest on $1,000 at 5% for one year is $(1,000)(.05) = $50. So you must compute the interest on $1,050 (not $1,000) for the second year. The interest is $(1,050)(.05) = 52.50. Therefore, during the third year interest will be computed for $1,102.50. During the third year the interest is $(1,102.50)(.05) = $55.125 = $55.13. Therefore, after 3 years the original $1,000 will be worth $1,157.63.

If you calculated simple interest on $1,000 at 5% for three years, the answer would be $(1,000)(.05)(3) = $150. Therefore, using simple interest, $1,000 is worth $1,150 after 3 years. Notice that this is not the same as the money was worth using compound interest.

You can assume that interest means simple interest unless a problem states otherwise.

The basic formula for discount problems is:

$$\text{DISCOUNT} = \text{COST} \times \text{RATE OF DISCOUNT}$$

EXAMPLE 1:

What is the discount if a car which cost $3,000 is discounted 7%?

The discount is $3,000 × .07 = $210 since 7% = .07.

If we know the cost of an item and its discounted price, we can find the rate of discount by using the formula

$$\text{rate of discount} = \frac{\text{cost} - \text{price}}{\text{cost}}.$$

After an item has been discounted once, it may be discounted again. This procedure is called *successive* discounting.

EXAMPLE 2:

A bicycle originally cost $100 and was discounted 10%. After three months it was sold after being discounted 15%. How much was the bicycle sold for?

After the 10% discount the bicycle was selling for $100 (.90) = $90. An item which costs $90 and is discounted 15% will sell for $90 (.85) = $76.50, so the bicycle was sold for $76.50.

Notice that if you added the two discounts of 10% and 15% and treated the successive discounts as a single discount of 25%, your answer would be that the bicycle sold for $75, which is incorrect. Successive discounts are not identical to a single discount of the sum of the discounts. The previous example shows that successive discounts of 10% and 15% are not identical to a single discount of 25%.

SIGNED NUMBERS

A number preceded by either a plus or a minus sign is called a *signed number*. For example, +5, –6, –4.2, and +¾ are all signed numbers. If no sign is given with a number, a plus sign is assumed; thus, 5 is interpreted as +5.

Signed numbers can often be used to distinguish different concepts. For example, a profit of $10 can be denoted by +$10 and a loss of $10 by –$10. A temperature of 20 degees below zero can be denoted –20°.

Absolute Value

The absolute value of a signed number is the distance of the number from 0. The absolute value of any nonzero number is *positive*. For example, the absolute value of 2 is 2; the absolute value of –2 is 2. The absolute value of a number a is denoted by $|a|$, so $|-2| = 2$. The absolute value of any number can be found by dropping its sign, $|-12| = 12$, $|4| = 4$. *Thus $|-a| = |a|$ for any number a.* The only number whose absolute value is zero is zero.

Adding Signed Numbers

Case I. Adding numbers with the *same sign:*

    (A) The sign of the sum is the same as the sign of the numbers being added.

    (B) Add the absolute values.

    (C) Put the sign from step (A) in front of the number you obtained in step (B).

EXAMPLE 1:

What is $-2 + (-3.1) + (-.02)$?

(A) The sign of the sum will be $-$.

(B) $|-2| = 2, |-3.1| = 3.1, |-.02| = .02$, and $2 + 3.1 + .02 = 5.12$.

(C) The answer is -5.12.

Case II. Adding two numbers with _different signs_:

(A) The sign of the sum is the sign of the number which is largest in absolute value.

(B) Subtract the absolute value of the number with the smaller absolute value from the absolute value of the number with the larger absolute value.

(C) The answer is the number you obtained in step (B) preceded by the sign from part (A).

EXAMPLE 2:

How much is $-5.1 + 3$?

(A) The absolute value of -5.1 is 5.1 and the absolute value of 3 is 3, so the sign of the sum will be $-$.

(B) 5.1 is larger than 3, and $5.1 - 3 = 2.1$.

(C) The sum is -2.1.

Case III. Adding _more than two_ numbers with _different_ signs:

(A) Add all the positive numbers; the result is positive (this is Case I).

(B) Add all the negative numbers, the result is negative (this is Case I).

(C) Add the result of step (A) to the result of step (B), by using Case II.

EXAMPLE 3:

Find the value of $5 + 52 + (-3) + 7 + (-5.1)$.

(A) $5 + 52 + 7 = 64$.

(B) $-3 + (-5.1) = -8.1$.

(C) $64 + (-8.1) = 55.9$, so the answer is 55.9.

Subtracting Signed Numbers

When subtracting signed numbers:

(A) Change the sign of the number you are subtracting (the subtrahend).

(B) <u>Add</u> the result of step (A) to the number being subtracted from (the minuend) using the rules of the preceding section.

EXAMPLE 1:

Subtract 4.1 from 6.5.

(A) 4.1 becomes −4.1.

(B) $6.5 + (−4.1) = 2.4$.

EXAMPLE 2:

What is $7.8 − (−10.1)$?

(A) −10.1 becomes 10.1.

(B) $7.8 + 10.1 = 17.9$.

So we subtract a negative number by adding a positive number with the same absolute value, and we subtract a positive number by adding a negative number of the same absolute value.

Multiplying Signed Numbers

Case I. Multiplying two numbers:

(A) Multiply the absolute values of the numbers.

(B) If both numbers have the same sign, the result of step (A) is the answer—i.e., the product is positive. If the numbers have different signs, then the answer is the result of step (A) with a minus sign.

EXAMPLE 1:

$(4)(−3) = ?$

(A) $4 × 3 = 12$

(B) The signs are different, so the answer is −12. You can

remember the sign of the product in the following way:

$$(-)(-) = +$$
$$(+)(+) = +$$
$$(-)(+) = -$$
$$(+)(-) = -$$

Case II. Multiplying more than two numbers:

(A) Multiply the first two factors using Case I.
(B) Multiply the result of (A) by the third factor.
(C) Multiply the result of (B) by the fourth factor.
(D) Continue until you have used each factor.

EXAMPLE 2:

$(-5)(4)(2)\left(-\frac{1}{2}\right)\left(\frac{3}{4}\right) = ?$

(A) $(-5)(4) = -20$

(B) $(-20)(2) = -40$

(C) $(-40)\left(-\frac{1}{2}\right) = 20$

$\frac{3}{4}$ (D) $(20)(\ \ ) = 15$, so the ans

The sign of the product is + if there are no negative factors or an even number of negative factors. The sign of the product is – if there is an odd number of negative factors.

Dividing Signed Numbers

Divide the absolute values of the numbers; the sign of the quotient is determined by the same rules as you used to determine the sign of a product. Thus,

$$+ \div + = +$$
$$- \div - = +$$
$$+ \div - = -$$
$$- \div + = -$$

EXAMPLE:

Divide 53.2 by –4.

53.2 divided by 4 is 13.3. Since one of the numbers is positive and the other negative, the answer is –13.3.

AVERAGES AND MEDIANS

Mean

The *average* or *arithmetic mean* of a collection of N numbers is the result of dividing the sum of all the numbers in the collection by N.

EXAMPLE:

The scores of 9 students on a test were 72, 78, 81, 64, 85, 92, 95, 60, and 55. What was the average score of the students?

Since there are 9 students, the average is the total of all the scores divided by 9.

So the average is $\frac{1}{9}$ of $(72+78+81+64+85+92+95+60+55)$,

which is $\frac{1}{9}$ of 682 or $75\frac{7}{9}$.

Median

The number that is in the middle, if the numbers in a collection of numbers are arranged in chronological order, is called the *median*. In the example above, the median score was 78. Notice that the median was different from the average.

> In general, the median and the average of a collection of numbers are different.

If the number of objects in the collection is even, the median is the average of the two numbers in the middle of the array. For example, the median of 64, 66, 72, 75, 76, and 77 is the average of 72 and 75, which is 73.5.

POWERS, EXPONENTS, AND ROOTS

If b is any number and n is a whole number greater than 0, b^n means the product of n factors, each of which is equal to b. Thus,

$b^n = b \times b \times b \times \ldots \times b$, where there are n copies of b.

If $n = 1$, there is only one copy of b, so $b^1 = b$. Here are some examples:

$$2^5 = 2 \times 2 \times 2 \times 2 \times 2 = 32, \; (-4)^3 = (-4) \times (-4) \times (-4) = -64,$$

$$\frac{3^2}{4} = \frac{3 \times 3}{4} = \frac{9}{4},$$

$$1^n = 1 \text{ for any } n, \; 0^n = 0 \text{ for any } n.$$

b^n is read as "b raised to the nth power." b^2 is read "b squared." b^2 is always greater than 0 (positive) if b is not zero, since the product of two negative numbers is positive. b^3 is read "b cubed." b^3 can be negative or positive.

If you raise a fraction, $\frac{p}{q}$, to a power, then $\left(\frac{p}{q} \right)^n = \frac{p^n}{q^n}$. For example,

$$\left(\frac{5}{4} \right)^3 = \frac{5^3}{4^3} = \frac{125}{64}$$

Exponents

In the expression b^n, b is called the *base* and n is called the *exponent*. In the expression 2^5, 2 is the base and 5 is the exponent. The exponent tells how many factors there are.

> *The two basic formulas for problems involving exponents are:*
> (A) $b^n \times b^m = b^{n+m}$
> (B) $a^n \times b^n = (a \cdot b)^n$
> (A) and (B) are called *laws of exponents.*

EXAMPLE:
What is 6^3?

Since $6 = 3 \times 2$, $6^3 = 3^3 \times 2^3 = 27 \times 8 = 216$.

or

$$6^3 = 6 \times 6 \times 6 = 216$$

Roots

If you raise a number d to the nth power and the result is b, then d is called the nth root of b, which is usually written $\sqrt[n]{b} = d$. Since $2^5 = 32$, then $\sqrt[5]{32} = 2$. The second root is called the square root and is written $\sqrt{\ }$; the third root is called the cube root. For example, $\sqrt{225} = 15$; $\sqrt{81} = 9$; $\sqrt[3]{64} = 4$.

There are two possibilities for the square root of a positive number; the positive one is called the square root. Thus we say $\sqrt{9} = 3$ although $(-3) \times (-3) = 9$.

Since the square of any nonzero number is positive, *the square root of a negative number is not defined as a real number.* Thus $\sqrt{-2}$ is not a real number. There are cube roots of negative numbers. $\sqrt[3]{-8} = -2$, because $(-2) \times (-2) \times (-2) = -8$.

You can also write roots as exponents; for example,

$$\sqrt[n]{b} = b^{\frac{1}{n}}; \text{ so } \sqrt{b} = b^{\frac{1}{2}}, \sqrt[3]{b} \ b^{\frac{1}{3}}.$$

Since you can write roots as exponents, formula (B) above is especially useful.

$$a^{\frac{1}{n}} \times b^{\frac{1}{n}} = (a \cdot b)^{\frac{1}{n}} \text{ or } \sqrt[n]{a \times b} = \sqrt[n]{a} \times \sqrt[n]{b}$$

This is the basic formula for simplifying square roots, cube roots, and so on. *On the test you must state your answer in a form that matches one of the choices given.*

EXAMPLE:

$\sqrt{54} = ?$

Since $54 = 9 \times 6$, $\sqrt{54} = \sqrt{9 \times 6} = \sqrt{9} \times \sqrt{6}$. Since $\sqrt{9} = 3$, $\sqrt{54} = 3\sqrt{6}$.

You cannot simplify by adding square roots unless you are taking square roots of the same number. For example, $\sqrt{3} + 2\sqrt{3} - 4\sqrt{3} = -\sqrt{3}$, but $\sqrt{3} + \sqrt{2}$ is not equal to $\sqrt{5}$.

ALGEBRA

ALGEBRAIC EXPRESSIONS

Often it is necessary to deal with quantities which have a numerical value which is unknown. For example, we may know that Tom's salary is twice as much as Joe's salary. If we let the value of Tom's salary be called T and the value of Joe's salary be J, then T and J are numbers which are unknown. However, we do know that the value of T must be twice the value of J, or $T = 2J$.

T and $2J$ are examples of algebraic expressions. An algebraic expression may involve letters in addition to numbers and symbols; however, *in an algebraic expression a letter always stands for a number*. Therefore, you can multiply, divide, add, subtract and perform other mathematical operations on a letter. Thus, x^2 would mean x times x. Some examples of algebraic expressions are: $2x + y$, $y^3 + 9y$, $z^3 - 5ab$, $c + d + 4$, $5x + 2y(6x - 4y + z)$. When letters or numbers are written together without any sign or symbol between them, multiplication is assumed. Thus $6xy$ means 6 times x times y. $6xy$ is called a term; terms are separated by $+$ or $-$ signs. The expression $5z + 2 + 4x^2$ has three terms, $5z$, 2, and $4x^2$. Terms are often called monomials (mono = one). If an expression has more than one term, it is called a *polynomial* (poly = many). The letters in an algebraic expression are called *variables* or *unknowns*. When a variable is multiplied by a number, the number is called the *coefficient* of the variable. So in the expression $5x^2 + 2yz$, the coefficient of x^2 is 5, and the coefficient of yz is 2.

Simplifying Algebraic Expressions

Since there are only five choices of an answer given for the test questions, you must be able to recognize algebraic expressions that are equal. It will also save time when you are working problems if you can change a complicated expression into a simpler one.

Case I. Simplifying expressions that don't contain parentheses:

(A) Perform any multiplications or divisions before performing additions or subtractions. Thus, the expression $6x + y \div x$ means add $6x$ to the quotient of y divided by x. Another way of writing the expression would be $6x + \dfrac{y}{x}$. This is not the same as $\dfrac{6x + y}{x}$.

(B) The order in which you multiply numbers and letters in a term does not matter. So $6xy$ is the same as $6yx$.

(C) The order in which you add terms does not matter; for instance, $6x + 2y - x = 6x - x + 2y$.

(D) If there are roots or powers in any terms, you may be able to simplify the term by using the laws of exponents. For example, $5xy \cdot 3x^2y = 15x^3y^2$.

(E) Combine like terms. *Like terms* (or similar terms) are terms which have exactly the same letters raised to the same powers. So x, $-2x$, $\frac{1}{3}x$ are like terms. For example, $6x - 2x + x + y$ is equal to $5x + y$. In combining like terms, you simply add or subtract the coefficients of the like terms, and the result is the coefficient of that term in the simplified expression. In the example given, the coefficients of x were $+6$, -2, and $+1$; since $6 - 2 + 1 = 5$, the coefficient of x in the simplified expression is 5.

(F) Algebraic expressions which involve divisions or factors can be simplified by using the techniques for handling fractions and the laws of exponents. Remember, dividing by b^n is the same as multiplying by b^{-n}.

EXAMPLE 1:

$3x^2 - 4\sqrt{x} + \sqrt{4x} + xy + 7x^2 = ?$

(D) $\sqrt{4x} = \sqrt{4}\sqrt{x} = 2\sqrt{x}$.

(E) $3x^2 + 7x^2 = 10x^2$, $-4\sqrt{x} + 2\sqrt{x} = -2\sqrt{x}$.

The original expression equals $3x^2 + 7x^2 - 4\sqrt{x} + 2\sqrt{x} + xy$. Therefore, the simplified expression is $10x^2 - 2\sqrt{x} + xy$.

Case II. Simplifying expressions that have parentheses:

The first rule is to perform the operations inside parentheses first. So $(6x + y) \div x$ means divide the sum of $6x$ and y by x. Notice that $(6x + y) \div x$ is different from $6x + y \div x$.

The main rule for getting rid of parentheses is the distributive law, which is expressed as $a(b + c) = ab + ac$. In other words, if any monomial is followed by an expression contained in parentheses, then *each* term of the expression is multiplied by the monomial. Once we have gotten rid of the parentheses, we proceed as we did in Case 1.

> If an expression has more than one set of parentheses, get rid of the *inner parentheses first* and then *work out* through the rest of the parentheses.

EXAMPLE 2:

$2x - (x + 6(x - 3y) + 4y) = ?$

To remove the inner parentheses we multiply $6(x - 3y)$, getting $6x - 18y$. Now we have $2x - (x + 6x - 18y + 4y)$, which equals $2x - (7x - 14y)$. Distribute the minus sign (multiply by -1), getting $2x - 7x - (-14y) = -5x + 14y$. Sometimes brackets are used instead of parentheses.

Adding and Subtracting Algebraic Expressions

Since algebraic expressions are numbers, they can be added and subtracted.

> *The only algebraic terms which can be combined are like terms.*

EXAMPLE:

$(3x + 4y - xy^2) + (3x + 2x(x - y)) = ?$

The expression $= (3x + 4y - xy^2) + (3x + 2x^2 - 2xy)$, removing the inner parentheses;

$= 6x + 4y + 2x^2 - xy^2 - 2xy$, combining like terms.

Multiplying Algebraic Expressions

When you multiply two expressions, you multiply *each term of the first by each term of the second.*

EXAMPLE 1:

$(2h - 4)(h + 2h^2 + h^3) = ?$
$= 2h(h + 2h^2 + h^3) - 4(h + 2h^2 + h^3)$
$= 2h^2 + 4h^3 + 2h^4 - 4h - 8h^2 - 4h^3$
$= -4h - 6h^2 + 2h^4$, which is the product.

If you need to multiply more than two expressions, multiply the first two expressions, then multiply the result by the third expression, and so on until you have used each factor. Since algebraic expressions can be multiplied, they can be squared, cubed, or raised to other powers.

EXAMPLE 2:

$(x - 2y)^3 = (x - 2y)(x - 2y)(x - 2y).$

Since $(x - 2y)(x - 2y) = x^2 - 2yx - 2yx + 4y^2$
$= x^2 - 4xy + 4y^2$
$(x - 2y)^3 = (x^2 - 4xy + 4y^2)(x - 2y)$
$= x(x^2 - 4xy + 4y^2) - 2y(x^2 - 4xy + 4y^2)$
$= x^3 - 4x^2y + 4xy^2 - 2x^2y + 8xy^2 - 8y^3$
$= x^3 - 6x^2y + 12xy^2 - 8y^3.$

The order in which you multiply algebraic expressions does not matter. Thus $(2a + b)(x^2 + 2x) = (x^2 + 2x)(2a + b)$.

Factoring Algebraic Expressions

If an algebraic expression is the product of other algebraic expressions, then the expressions are called factors of the original expression. For instance, we claim that $(2h - 4)$ and $(h + 2h^2 + h^3)$ are factors of $-4h - 6h^2 + 2h^4$. We can always check to see if we have the correct factors by multiplying; so by example 1 above we see that our claim is correct. We need to be able to factor algebraic expressions in order to solve quadratic equations. It also can be helpful in dividing algebraic expressions.

First remove any monomial factor which appears in every term of the expression. Some examples:

$3x + 3y = 3(x + y)$: 3 is a monomial factor.

$15a^2b + 10ab = 5ab(3a + 2)$: $5ab$ is a monomial factor.

$$\frac{1}{2}hy - 3h^3 + 4hy = h\left(\frac{1}{2}y - 3h^2 + 4y\right).$$

$$= h\left(\frac{9}{2}y - 3h^2\right)\text{: } h \text{ is a monomial factor.}$$

You may also need to factor expressions which contain squares or higher powers into factors which only contain linear terms. (Linear terms are terms in which variables are raised only to the first power.) The first rule to remember is that since $(a + b)(a - b) = a^2 + ba - ba - b^2 = a^2 - b^2$, the difference of two squares can always be factored.

EXAMPLE 1:

Factor $(9m^2 - 16)$.

$9m^2 = (3m)^2$ and $16 = 4^2$, so the factors are $(3m - 4)(3m + 4)$. Since $(3m - 4)(3m + 4) = 9m^2 - 16$, these factors are correct.

You also may need to factor expressions which contain squared terms and linear terms, such as $x^2 + 4x + 3$. The factors will be of the form $(x + a)$ and $(x + b)$. Since $(x + a)(x + b) = x^2 + (a + b)x + ab$, you must look for a pair of numbers a and b such that $a \cdot b$ is the numerical term in the expression and $a + b$ is the coefficient of the linear term (the term with exponent 1).

EXAMPLE 2:

Factor $y^2 + y - 6$.

Since -6 is negative, the two numbers a and b must be of opposite sign. Possible pairs of factors for -6 are -6 and $+1$, 6 and -1, 3 and -2, and -3 and 2. Since $-2 + 3 = 1$, the factors are $(y + 3)$ and $(y - 2)$. So $(y + 3)(y - 2) = y^2 + y - 6$.

There are some expressions which cannot be factored, for example, $x^2 + 4x + 6$. In general, if you can't factor something by using the methods given above, don't waste a lot of time on the question. Sometimes you may be able to check the answers given to find out what the correct factors are.

Dividing Algebraic Expressions

The main things to remember in division are:

(1) When you divide a sum, you can get the same result by dividing each term and adding quotients. For example,

$$\frac{9x + 4xy + y^2}{x} = \frac{9x}{x} + \frac{4xy}{x} + \frac{y^2}{x} = 9 + 4y + \frac{y^2}{x}.$$

(2) You can cancel common factors, so the results on factoring will be helpful. For example,

$$\frac{x^2 - 2x}{x - 2} = \frac{x(x - 2)}{x - 2} = x.$$

EQUATIONS

An *equation* is a statement that says two algebraic expressions are equal. $x + 2 = 3$, $4 + 2 = 6$, $3x^2 + 2x - 6 = 0$, $x^2 + y^2 = z^2$, $\frac{y}{x} = 2 + z$, and $A = LW$ are all examples of equations. We will refer to the algebraic expressions on each side of the equal sign as the left side or the right side of the equation. Thus, in the equation $2x + 4 = 6y + x$, $2x + 4$ is the left side and $6y + x$ is the right side.

If we assign specific numbers to each variable or unknown in an algebraic expression, then the algebraic expression will be equal to a number. This is called *evaluating* the expression. For example, if you evaluate $2x + 4y^2 + 3$ for $x = -1$ and $y = 2$, the expression is equal to $2(-1) + 4 \cdot 2^2 + 3 = -2 + 4 \cdot 4 + 3 = 17$.

If we evaluate each side of an equation and the number obtained is the same for each side of the equation, then the specific values assigned to the unknowns are called a *solution of the equation*. Another way of saying this is that the choices for the unknowns satisfy the equation.

EXAMPLE:

Consider the equation $x^2 + y^2 = 5x$.

If $x = 1$ and $y = 2$, then the left side is $1^2 + 2^2$, which equals $1 + 4 = 5$. The right side is $5 \cdot 1 = 5$; since both sides are equal to 5, $x = 1$ and $y = 2$ is a solution.

If $x = 1$ and $y = 1$, then the left side is $1^2 + 1^2 = 2$ and the right side is $5 \cdot 1 = 5$. Therefore, since $2 \neq 5$, $x = 1$ and $y = 1$ is not a solution.

There are some equations that *do not have any solutions that are real numbers*. Since the square of any real number is positive or zero, the equation $x^2 = -4$ does not have any solutions that are real numbers.

Equivalence

One equation is *equivalent* to another equation if they have exactly the same solutions. The basic idea in solving equations is to transform a given equation into an equivalent equation whose solutions are obvious.

The two main tools for solving equations are:

(A) If you add or subtract the same algebraic expression to or from *each side* of an equation, the resulting equation is equivalent to the original equation.

(B) If you multiply or divide both sides of an equation by the same *nonzero* algebraic expression, the resulting equation is equivalent to the original equation.

Solving Linear Equations with One Unknown

The most common type of equation is the linear equation with only one unknown. $6z = 4z - 3$, $3 + a = 2a - 4$, $3b + 2b = b - 4b$ are all examples of linear equations with only one unknown.

Using (A) and (B), you can solve a linear equation with one unknown in the following way:

(1) Group all the terms which involve the unknown on one side of the equation and all the terms which are purely numerical on the other side of the equation. This is called *isolating the unknown.*

(2) Combine the terms on each side.

(3) Divide each side by the coefficient of the unknown.

EXAMPLE 1:

Solve $3x + 15 = 3 - 4x$ for x.

(1) Add $4x$ to each side and subtract 15 from each side;
$3x + 15 - 15 + 4x = 3 - 15 - 4x + 4x.$

(2) $7x = -12.$

(3) Divide each side by 7 so $x = \dfrac{-12}{7}$ is the solution.

CHECK: $3\left(\dfrac{-12}{7}\right) + 15 = \dfrac{-36}{7} + 15 = \dfrac{69}{7}$

and $3 - 4\left(\dfrac{-12}{7}\right) = 3 + \dfrac{48}{7} = \dfrac{69}{7}.$

If you do the same thing to each side of an equation, the result is still an equation but it may not be equivalent to the original equation. Be especially careful if you square each side of an equation. For example, $x = -4$ is an equation; square both sides and you get $x^2 = 16$ which has both $x = 4$ and $x = -4$ as solutions. *Always check your answer in the original equation.*

If the equation you want to solve involves square roots, get rid of the square roots by squaring each side of the equation. Remember to check your answer since squaring each side does not always give an equivalent equation.

EXAMPLE 2:

Solve $\sqrt{4x + 3} = 5$.

Square both sides: $\left(\sqrt{4x + 3}\right)^2 = 4x + 3$ and $5^2 = 25$, so the new equation is $4x + 3 = 25$. Subtract 3 from each side to get $4x = 22$ and now divide each side by 4. The solution is $x = \frac{22}{4} = 5.5$. Since 4 (5.5) + 3 = 25 and $\sqrt{25} = 5$, $x = 5.5$ is a solution to the equation $\sqrt{4x + 3} = 5$.

If an equation involves fractions, multiply through by a common denominator and then solve. Check your answer to make sure you did not multiply or divide by zero.

Solving Two Equations with Two Unknowns

You may be asked to solve two equations with two unknowns. Use one equation to solve for one unknown in terms of the other; now change the second equation into an equation with only one unknown which can be solved by the methods of the preceding section.

EXAMPLE:

Solve for x and y: $\begin{cases} \dfrac{x}{y} = 3 \\ 2x + 4y = 20. \end{cases}$

The first equation gives $x = 3y$. Using $x = 3y$, the second equation is $2(3y) + 4y = 6y + 4y$ or $10y = 20$, so $y = \frac{20}{10} = 2$. Since $x = 3y$, $x = 6$.

CHECK: $\frac{6}{2} = 3$, and $2 \cdot 6 + 4 \cdot 2 = 20$, so $x = 6$ and $y = 2$ is a solution.

Solving Quadratic Equations

If the terms of an equation contain squares of the unknown as well as linear terms, the equation is called *quadratic*. Some examples of quadratic equations are $x^2 + 4x = 3$, $2z^2 - 1 = 3z^2 - 2z$, and $a + 6 = a^2 + 6$.

To solve a quadratic equation:

   (A) Group all the terms on one side of the equation so that the other side is *zero*.

   (B) Combine the terms on the nonzero side.

   (C) Factor the expression into linear expressions.

   (D) Set the linear factors equal to zero and solve.

The method depends on the fact that if a product of expressions is zero, then at least one of the expressions must be zero.

EXAMPLE:

Solve $x^2 + 4x = -3$.

   (A) $x^2 + 4x + 3 = 0$

   (C) $x^2 + 4x + 3 = (x + 3)(x + 1) = 0$

   (D) So $x + 3 = 0$ or $x + 1 = 0$. Therefore, the solutions are $x = -3$ and $x = -1$.

CHECK: $(-3)^2 + 4(-3) = 9 - 12 = -3$

        $(-1)^2 + 4(-1) = 1 - 4 = -3$, so $x = -3$ and $x = -1$ are solutions.

A quadratic equation will usually have 2 different solutions, but it is possible for a quadratic to have only one solution or even no real solution.

WORD PROBLEMS

The general method for solving word problems is to translate them into algebraic problems. The quantities you are seeking are the unknowns, which are usually represented by letters. The information you are given in the problem is then turned into equations. Words such as "is," "was," "are," and "were" mean equals, and words like "of" and "as much as" mean multiplication.

EXAMPLE 1:

A coat was sold for $75. The coat was sold for 150% of the cost of the coat. How much did the coat cost?

You want to find the cost of the coat. Let $\$C$ be the cost of the coat. You know that the coat was sold for $75 and that $75 was 150% of the cost. So $75 = 150\%$ of C or $75 = 1.5C$. Solving for C you get

$C = \dfrac{75}{1.5} = 50$, so the coat cost $50.

CHECK: $(1.5)\$50 = \$75$.

EXAMPLE 2:

Tom's salary is 125% of Joe's salary; Mary's salary is 80% of Joe's salary. The total of all three salaries is $61,000. What is Mary's salary?

Let $M =$ Mary's salary, $J =$ Joe's salary, and $T =$ Tom's salary. The first sentence says $T = 125\%$ of J or $T = \dfrac{5}{4} J$, and $M = 80\%$ of J

or $M = \dfrac{4}{5} J$. The second sentence says that $T + M + J = \$61,000$. Using

the information from the first sentence, $T + M + J = \dfrac{5}{4} J + \dfrac{4}{5} J + J =$

$\dfrac{25}{20} J + \dfrac{16}{20} J + J = \dfrac{61}{20} J$. So $\dfrac{61}{20} J = 61,000$; solving for J you have

$J = \dfrac{20}{61} \times 61,000 = 20,000$. Therefore, $T = \dfrac{5}{4} \times \$20,000 = \$25,000$

and $M = \dfrac{4}{5} \times \$20,000 = \$16,000$.

CHECK: $\$25,000 + \$16,000 + \$20,000 = \$61,000$.
So Mary's salary is $16,000.

EXAMPLE 3:

Steve weighs 25 pounds more than Jim. The combined weight of Jim and Steve is 325 pounds. How much does Jim weigh?

Let $S =$ Steve's weight in pounds and $J =$ Jim's weight in pounds. The first sentence says $S = J + 25$, and the second sentence becomes $S + J = 325$. Since $S = J + 25$, $S + J = 325$ becomes $(J + 25) + J = 2J + 25 = 325$. So $2J = 300$ and $J = 150$. Therefore, Jim weighs 150 pounds.

CHECK: If Jim weighs 150 pounds, then Steve weighs 175 pounds and $150 + 175 = 325$.

EXAMPLE 4:

A carpenter is designing a closet. The floor will be in the shape of a rectangle whose length is 2 feet more than its width. How long should the closet be if the carpenter wants the area of the floor to be 15 square feet?

The area of a rectangle is length times width, usually written $A = LW$, where A is the area, L is the length, and W is the width. We know $A = 15$ and $L = 2 + W$. Therefore, $LW = (2 + W)W = W^2 + 2W$; this must equal 15. So we need to solve $W^2 + 2W = 15$ or $W^2 + 2W - 15 = 0$. Since $W^2 + 2W - 15$ factors into $(W + 5)(W - 3)$, the only possible solutions are $W = -5$ and $W = 3$. Since W represents a width, -5 cannot be the answer; therefore the width is 3 feet. The length is the width plus two feet, so the length is 5 feet. Since $5 \times 3 = 15$, the answer checks.

Distance Problems

A common type of word problem is a distance or velocity problem. The basic formula is

$$\boxed{\text{DISTANCE TRAVELED} = \text{SPEED} \times \text{TIME}}$$

The formula is abbreviated $d = st$. Velocity or rate are other names for speed.

EXAMPLE:

A train travels at an average speed of 50 miles per hour for $2\frac{1}{2}$ hours and then travels at a speed of 70 miles per hour for $1\frac{1}{2}$ hours. How far did the train travel in the entire 4 hours?

The train traveled for $2\frac{1}{2}$ hours at an average speed of 50 miles per hour, so it traveled $50 \times \frac{5}{2} = 125$ miles in the first $2\frac{1}{2}$ hours.

Traveling at a speed of 70 miles per hour for $1\frac{1}{2}$ hours, the distance traveled will be equal to $s \times t$ where $s = 70$ m.p.h. and $t = 1\frac{1}{2}$, so the distance is $70 \times \frac{3}{2} = 105$ miles. Therefore, the total distance traveled is $125 + 105 = 230$ miles.

Work Problems

In this type of problem you can always assume all workers in the same category work at the same rate. The main idea is: If it takes k workers 1 hour to do a job, then *each worker does* $\frac{1}{k}$ *of the job in an hour* or she works at the rate of $\frac{1}{k}$ of the job per hour. If it takes m workers h hours to finish a job then each worker does $\frac{1}{m}$ of the job in h hours so she does $\frac{1}{h}$ of $\frac{1}{m}$ in an hour. Therefore, each worker *works at the rate of* $\frac{1}{hm}$ *of the job per hour.*

EXAMPLE:

If 5 men take an hour to dig a ditch, how long should it take 12 men to dig a ditch of the same type?

Since 5 workers took an hour, each worker does $\frac{1}{5}$ of the job in an hour. So 12 workers will work at the rate of $\frac{12}{5}$ of the job per hour.

Thus if T is the time it takes for 12 workers to do the job, $\frac{12}{5} \times T = 1$

job and $T = \frac{5}{12} \times 1$, so $T = \frac{5}{12}$ hour or 25 minutes.

INEQUALITIES

A number is positive if it is greater than 0, so 1, $\frac{1}{1,000}$, and 53.4 are

all positive numbers. Positive numbers are signed numbers whose sign is +. If you think of numbers as points on a number line, positive numbers correspond to points to the right of 0.

A number is negative if it is less than 0. $-\frac{4}{5}$, −50, and −.0001

are all negative numbers. Negative numbers are signed numbers whose sign is −. Negative numbers correspond to points to the left of 0 on a number line.

0 is the only number which is neither positive nor negative.

$a > b$ means the number a is greater than the number b; that is, $a = b + x$ where x is a positive number. If we look at a number line, $a > b$ means a is to the right of b. $a > b$ can also be read as b is less than a, which is also written $b < a$. For example, $-5 > -7.5$ because $-5 = -7.5 + 2.5$ and 2.5 is positive.

The notation $a \le b$ means a is less than or equal to b, or b is greater than or equal to a. For example, $5 \ge 4$; also $4 \ge 4$. $a \ne b$ means a is not equal to b.

If you need to know whether one fraction is greater than another fraction, put the fractions over a common denominator and compare the numerators.

EXAMPLE:

Which is larger, $\frac{13}{16}$ or $\frac{31}{40}$?

A common denominator is 80. $\dfrac{13}{16} = \dfrac{65}{80}$, and $\dfrac{31}{40} = \dfrac{62}{80}$; since

$65 > 62$, $\dfrac{65}{80} > \dfrac{62}{80}$, so $\dfrac{13}{16} > \dfrac{31}{40}$.

Inequalities have certain properties which are similar to equations. We can talk about the left side and the right side of an inequality, and we can use algebraic expressions for the sides of an inequality. For example, $6x < 5x + 4$. A value for an unknown *satisfies an inequality* if when you evaluate each side of the inequality the numbers satisfy the inequality. So if $x = 2$, then $6x = 12$ and $5x + 4 = 14$, and since $12 < 14$, $x = 2$ satisfies $6x < 5x + 4$. Two inequalities are equivalent if the same collection of numbers satisfies both inequalities.

The following basic principles are used in work with inequalities:

(A) Adding the same expression to *each* side of an inequality gives an equivalent inequality (written $a < b \leftrightarrow a + c < b + c$ where $\leftrightarrow$ means equivalent).

(B) Subtracting the same expression from *each* side of an inequality gives an equivalent inequality ($a < b \leftrightarrow a - c < b - c$).

(C) Multiplying or dividing *each* side of an inequality by the same *positive* expression gives an equivalent inequality ($a < b \leftrightarrow ca < cb$ for $c > 0$).

(D) Multiplying or dividing each side of an inequality by the same *negative* expression *reverses* the inequality ($a < b \leftrightarrow ca > cb$ for $c < 0$).

(E) If both sides of an inequality have the same sign, inverting both sides of the inequality *reverses* the inequality.

$$0 < a < b \leftrightarrow 0 < \dfrac{1}{b} < \dfrac{1}{a}$$

$$a < b < 0 \leftrightarrow \dfrac{1}{b} < \dfrac{1}{a} < 0$$

(F) If two inequalities are of the same type (both greater or both less), adding the respective sides gives the same type of inequality.

($a < b$ and $c < d$, then $a + c < b + d$)

Note that the inequalities are *not* equivalent.

(G) If $a < b$ and $b < c$, then $a < c$.

EXAMPLE 1:

Find the values of x for which $5x - 4 < 7x + 2$.

Using principle (B) subtract $5x + 2$ from each side, so $(5x - 4 < 7x + 2) \leftrightarrow -6 < 2x$. Now use principle (C) and divide each side by 2, so $-6 < 2x \leftrightarrow -3 < x$.

So any x greater than -3 satisfies the inequality. It is a good idea to make a spot check. -1 is > -3; let $x = -1$, then $5x - 4 = -9$ and $7x + 2 = -5$. Since $-9 < -5$, the answer is correct for at least the particular value $x = -1$.

EXAMPLE 2:

Find the values of a which satisfy $a^2 + 1 > 2a + 4$.

Subtract $2a$ from each side, so
$(a^2 + 1 > 2a + 4) \leftrightarrow a^2 - 2a + 1 > 4$.
$a^2 - 2a + 1 = (a - 1)^2$, so
$a^2 - 2a + 1 > 4 \leftrightarrow (a - 1)^2 > 2^2$.

We need to be careful when we take the square roots of inequalities. If $q^2 > 4$ and if $q > 0$, then $q > 2$; but if $q < 0$, then $q < -2$. We must look at two cases in example 2. First, if $(a - 1) \geq 0$, then

$(a - 1)^2 > 2^2 \leftrightarrow a - 1 > 2$ or $a > 3$.
If $(a - 1) < 0$ then $(a - 1)^2 > 2^2 \leftrightarrow a - 1 < -2 \leftrightarrow a < -1$.
So the inequality is satisfied if $a > 3$ or if $a < -1$.

CHECK: $(-2)^2 + 1 = 5 > 2(-2) + 4 = 0$, and $5^2 + 1 = 26 > 14 = 2 \cdot 5 + 4$.

Some inequalities are not satisfied by *any* real number. For example, since $x^2 \geq 0$ for all x, there is no real number x such that $x^2 < -9$.

You may be given an inequality and asked whether other inequalities follow from the original inequality. You should be able to answer such questions by using principles (A) through (G).

If there is any property of inequalities you can't remember, try out some specific numbers. If $x < y$, then what is the relation between $-x$ and $-y$? Since $4 < 5$ but $-5 < -4$, the relation is probably $-x > -y$, which is true by (D).

Probably the most common mistake is forgetting to reverse the inequalities if you multiply or divide by a negative number.

GEOMETRY

ANGLES

If two straight lines meet at a point they form an *angle*. The point is called the *vertex* of the angle and the lines are called the *sides* or *rays* of the angle. The sign for angle is $\angle$.

If two lines intersect at a point, they form 4 angles. The angles opposite each other are called *vertical* angles. $\angle 1$ and $\angle 3$ are vertical angles. $\angle 2$ and $\angle 4$ are vertical angles.

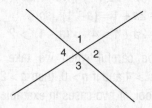

Vertical angles are equal.

A straight angle is an angle whose sides lie on a straight line. *A straight angle equals 180°.*

If the sum of two adjacent angles is a straight angle, then the angles are *supplementary* and each angle is the supplement of the other.

If an angle of $x°$ and an angle of $y°$ are supplements, then $x + y = 180$.

If two supplementary angles are equal, they are both *right angles*. A right angle is half of a straight angle. A right angle $= 90°$.

If the sum of two adjacent angles is a right angle, then the angles are *complementary* and each angle is the complement of the other.

If an angle of $x°$ and an angle of $y°$ are complementary, then $x + y = 90$.

LINES

A line is understood to be a straight line. A line is assumed to extend indefinitely in both directions. *There is one and only one line between two distinct points.*

Parallel Lines

Two lines in the same plane are *parallel* if they do not intersect no matter how far they are extended.

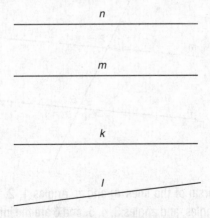

m and n are parallel, but k and l are not parallel since if k and l are extended they will intersect. Parallel lines are denoted by the symbol ||; so $m \parallel n$ means m is parallel to n.

If two lines are parallel to a third line, then they are parallel to each other.

If a third line intersects two given lines, it is called a *transversal*. A transversal and the two given lines form eight angles. The four inside angles are called *interior* angles. The four outside angles are called *exterior* angles. If two angles are on opposite sides of the transversal they are called *alternate* angles.

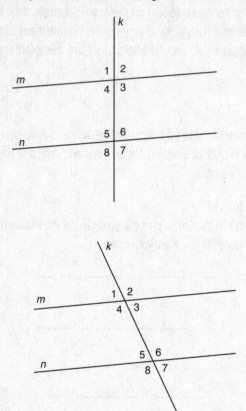

k is a transversal of the lines m and n. Angles 1, 2, 7, and 8 are the exterior angles, and angles 3, 4, 5, and 6 are the interior angles. $\angle 4$ and $\angle 6$ are an example of a pair of alternate angles. $\angle 1$ and $\angle 5$, $\angle 2$ and $\angle 6$, $\angle 3$ and $\angle 7$, and $\angle 4$ and $\angle 8$ are pairs of *corresponding* angles.

If two parallel lines are intersected by a transversal, then:
  (1) Alternate interior angles are equal.
  (2) Corresponding angles are equal.
  (3) Interior angles on the same side of the transversal
       are supplementary.

If we use the fact that vertical angles are equal, we can replace "interior" by "exterior" in (1) and (3).

Perpendicular Lines

When two lines intersect and all four of the angles formed are equal, the lines are said to be *perpendicular*. If two lines are perpendicular, they are the sides of right angles whose vertex is the point of intersection.

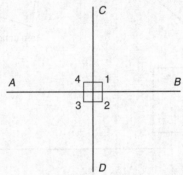

AB is perpendicular to *CD*, and angles 1, 2, 3, and 4 are all right angles. ⊥ is the symbol for perpendicular; so *AB* ⊥ *CD*.

If *any one* of the angles formed when two lines intersect is a right angle, then the lines are perpendicular.

POLYGONS

A *polygon* is a closed figure in a plane which is composed of line segments which meet only at their endpoints. The line segments are called *sides* of the polygon, and a point where two sides meet is called a *vertex* (plural *vertices*) of the polygon.

Polygons are classified by the number of angles or sides they have. A polygon with three angles is called a *triangle;* a four-sided polygon is a *quadrilateral;* a polygon with five angles is a *pentagon;* a polygon with six angles is a *hexagon;* an eight-sided polygon is an *octagon.* The number of angles is always equal to the number of sides in a polygon, so a six-sided polygon is a hexagon. The term *n*-gon refers to a polygon with *n* sides.

If the corresponding sides and the corresponding angles of two polygons are equal, the polygons are *congruent.* Congruent polygons have the same size and the same shape.

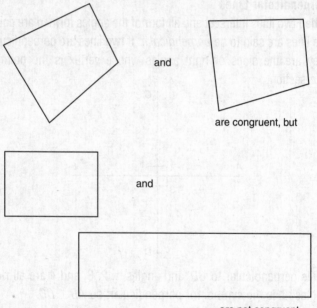

and

are congruent, but

and

are not congruent.

The sum of all the angles of an *n*-gon is $(n - 2)180°$. So the sum of the angles in a hexagon is $(6 - 2)180° = 720°$.

TRIANGLES

A *triangle* is a 3-sided polygon. If two sides of a triangle are equal, it is called *isosceles.* If all three sides are equal, it is an *equilateral* triangle. The symbol for a triangle is $\triangle$; so $\triangle ABC$ means a triangle whose vertices are *A, B,* and *C.*

The sum of the angles in a triangle is 180°.

The sum of the lengths of any two sides of a triangle must be longer than the remaining side.

If two angles in a triangle are equal, then the lengths of the sides opposite the equal angles are equal. If two sides of a triangle are equal, then the angles opposite the two equal sides are equal. In an equilateral triangle all the angles are equal and each angle = 60°. If each of the angles in a triangle is 60°, then the triangle is equilateral.

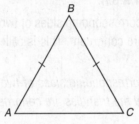

If $AB = BC$, then $\angle BAC = \angle BCA$.

In a right triangle, the side opposite the right angle is called the *hypotenuse,* and the remaining two sides are called legs.

The Pythagorean Theorem states that the square of the length of the hypotenuse is equal to the sum of the squares of the lengths of the legs.

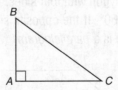

$(BC)^2 = (AB)^2 + (AC)^2$

If $AB = 4$ and $AC = 3$, then $(BC)^2 = 4^2 + 3^2 = 25$, so $BC = 5$. If $BC = 13$ and $AC = 5$, then $13^2 = 169 = (AB)^2 + 5^2$. So $(AB)^2 = 169 - 25 = 144$ and $AB = 12$.

If the lengths of the three sides of a triangle are a, b, and c and $a^2 + b^2 = c^2$, then the triangle is a right triangle where c is the length of the hypotenuse.

Congruence

Two triangles are congruent if two pairs of corresponding sides and the corresponding *included* angles are equal. This is called *Side-Angle-Side* and is denoted by S.A.S.

Two triangles are congruent if two pairs of corresponding angles and the corresponding *included* sides are equal. This is called *Angle-Side-Angle* or A.S.A.

If all three pairs of corresponding sides of two triangles are equal, then the triangles are congruent. This is called *Side-Side-Side* or S.S.S.

In general, if two corresponding sides of two triangles are equal, we cannot infer that the triangles are congruent.

The symbol $\cong$ means congruent.

Similarity

Two triangles are similar if all three pairs of corresponding angles are equal. Since the sum of the angles in a triangle is 180°, it follows that if two corresponding angles are equal, the third angles must be equal. The symbol $\sim$ means similar.

QUADRILATERALS

A *quadrilateral* is a polygon with four sides. The sum of the angles in a quadrilateral is 360°. If the opposite sides of a quadrilateral are parallel, the figure is a *parallelogram*.

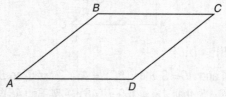

ABCD is a parallelogram.

In a parallelogram:

  (1) Opposite sides are equal.
  (2) Opposite angles are equal.
  (3) All diagonals divide the parallelogram into two
       congruent triangles.
  (4) The diagonals bisect each other. (A line *bisects* a line
       segment if it intersects the segment at the midpoint of
       the segment.)

If *any* of the statements (1), (2), (3), and (4) are true for a quadrilateral, then the quadrilateral is a parallelogram.

If all the angles of a parallelogram are right angles, the figure is a *rectangle*.

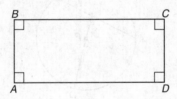

ABCD is a rectangle.

Since the sum of the angles in a quadrilateral is 360°, if *all* the angles of a quadrilateral are equal, then the figure is a rectangle. The diagonals of a rectangle are equal. The length of a diagonal can be found by using the Pythagorean theorem.

If all the sides of a rectangle are equal, the figure is a *square*.

A quadrilateral with two parallel sides and two sides that are not parallel is called a *trapezoid*. The parallel sides are called bases, and the nonparallel sides are called legs.

If *BC* ‖ *AD,* then *ABCD* is a trapezoid; *BC* and *AD* are the bases.

CIRCLES

A *circle* is a figure in a plane consisting of all the points which are the same distance from a fixed point called the *center* of the circle. A line segment from any point on the circle to the center of the circle is called a *radius* (plural: *radii*) of the circle. All radii of the same circle have the same length.

A line segment whose endpoints are on a circle is called a *chord*. A chord which passes through the center of the circle is a *diameter*. *The length of a diameter is twice the length of a radius.* A diameter divides a circle into two congruent halves which are called *semi-circles*.

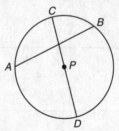

P is the center of the circle.
AB is a chord, *CD* is a diameter, and *PC* and *PD* are radii.

A diameter which is perpendicular to a chord bisects the chord.

If a line intersects a circle at one and only one point, the line is said to be a *tangent* to the circle. The point common to a circle and a tangent to the circle is called the *point of tangency*. The radius from the center to the point of tangency is perpendicular to the tangent.

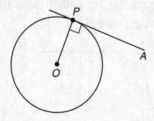

AP is tangent to the circle with center *O*. *P* is the point of tangency and *OP* ⊥ *PA*.

An angle whose vertex is a point on a circle and whose sides are chords of the circle is called an *inscribed angle.* An angle whose vertex is the center of a circle and whose sides are radii of the circle is called a *central angle.*

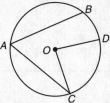

∠*BAC* is an inscribed angle.
∠*DOC* is a central angle.

An *arc* is a part of a circle.

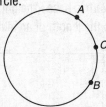

ACB is an arc. Arc *ACB* is written $\overgroup{ACB}$.

An arc can be measured in degrees. The entire circle is 360°, thus an arc of 120° would be $\frac{1}{3}$ of a circle.

A central angle is equal in measure to the arc it intercepts.

An inscribed angle is equal in measure to $\frac{1}{2}$ the arc it intercepts.

AREA AND PERIMETER

Area

The *area of a square* equals s^2, where s is the length of a side of the square. Thus, $A = s^2$.

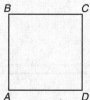

If *AD* = 5 inches, the area of square *ABCD* is 25 square inches.

The *area of a rectangle* equals length times width; if *L* is the length of one side and *W* is the length of a perpendicular side, then the area is $A = LW$.

If $AB = 5$ feet and $AD = 8$ feet, then the area of rectangle *ABCD* is 40 square feet.

The *area of a parallelogram* is base × height; $A = bh$, where *b* is the length of a side and *h* is the length of an altitude to the base.

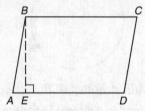

If $AD = 6$ yards and $BE = 4$ yards, then the area of the parallelogram *ABCD* is 6 · 4 or 24 square yards.

The *area of a trapezoid* is the (average of the bases) × height. $A = [(b_1 + b_2)/2]h$, where b_1 and b_2 are the lengths of the parallel sides and *h* is the length of an altitude to one of the bases.

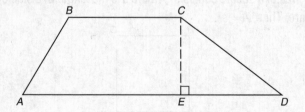

If $BC = 3$ miles, $AD = 7$ miles, and $CE = 2$ miles, then the area of trapezoid $ABCD$ is $[(3 + 7)/2] \cdot 2 = 10$ square miles.

The *area of a triangle* is $\frac{1}{2}$ (base × height); $A = \frac{1}{2} bh$, where b is the length of a side and h is the length of the altitude to that side.

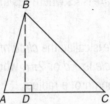

If $AC = 5$ miles and $BD = 4$ miles, then the area of the triangle is $\frac{1}{2} \times 5 \times 4 = 10$ square miles.

If we want to find the *area of a polygon* which is not of a type already mentioned, we break the polygon up into smaller figures such as triangles or rectangles, find the area of each piece, and add these to get the area of the given polygon.

The *area of a circle* is πr^2, where r is the length of a radius. Since $d = 2r$ where d is the length of a diameter, $A = \pi \left(\frac{d}{2} \right)^2 = \pi \frac{d^2}{4}$. π is a number which is approximately $\frac{22}{7}$ or 3.14; however, there is *no fraction which is exactly equal to π. π is called an irrational number.*

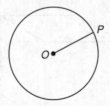

If $OP = 2$ inches, then the area of the circle with center O is $\pi 2^2$ or 4π square inches.

Perimeter

The *perimeter of a polygon* is the sum of the lengths of the sides.

The *perimeter of a rectangle* is $2(L + W)$, where L is the length and W is the width.

The *perimeter of a square* is $4s$ where s is the length of a side of the square.

The *perimeter of a circle* is called the *circumference* of the circle. The *circumference of a circle* is πd or $2\pi r$, where d is the length of a diameter and r is the length of a radius.

VOLUME AND SURFACE AREA

Volume

The *volume of a rectangular solid or box* is length times width times height.

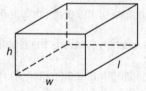

If each of the faces of a rectangular solid is a congruent square, then the solid is a *cube*. The *volume of a cube* is the length of a side (or edge) cubed.

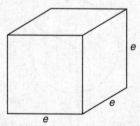

If the side of a cube is 4 feet long, then the volume of the cube is 4^3 or 64 cubic feet.

This solid is a circular cylinder. The top and the bottom are congruent circles. Most tin cans are circular cylinders. The *volume of a circular cylinder* is the product of the area of the circular base and the height.

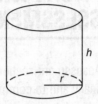

A *sphere* is the set of points in space equidistant from a fixed point called the center. The length of a segment from any point on the sphere to the center is called the radius of the sphere. *The volume of a sphere* of radius r is $\frac{4}{3}\pi r^3$.

The volume of a sphere with radius 3 feet is $\frac{4}{3}\pi 3^3 = 36\pi$ cubic feet.

Surface Area

The *surface area of a rectangular prism* is $2LW + 2LH + 2WH$, where L is the length, W is the width, and H is the height.

The *surface area of a cube* is $6e^2$, where e is the length of an edge.

The *area of the circular part of a cylinder* is called the lateral area. The *lateral area of a cylinder* is $2\pi rh$, since if we unroll the circular part we get a rectangle whose dimensions are the circumference of the circle and the height of the cylinder. The total surface area is the lateral surface area plus the areas of the circles on top and bottom, so the total surface area is $2\pi rh + 2\pi r^2$.

6
ANALYTICAL WRITING ASSESSMENT

The Analytical Writing Assessment section is designed to assess your ability to think critically and to communicate complex ideas. The writing task consists of two sections that require you to examine the composition of an issue, take a position on the basis of the details of the issue, and present a critique of the conclusion derived from a specific way of thinking. The issues are taken from topics of general interest related to business or to other subjects. There is no presumption of any specific knowledge about business or other areas.

The Analytical Writing Assessment is written on the computer, but it is the only part of the GMAT CAT that is not computer adaptive. The test taker writes two essays in response to questions.

There are two types of Analytical Writing Assessment tasks:

1. **Analysis of an issue**
2. **Analysis of an argument**

ANALYSIS OF AN ISSUE

Some analysts complain that consumers do not receive enough information to make rational purchase decisions. When the consumer is unable to make rational decisions, the economy suffers. Behavioral scientists contend that emotional and psychological factors play an important role in the satisfaction of consumer wants and that the measurable quantitative information being proposed by others is not as relevant for consumer decision-making as purported to be.

Which do you find more convincing: the complaint of the analysts or the contention of the behavioral scientists? State your position using relevant reasons and examples from your own experience, observation, or reading.

TEST-TAKING TIPS

1. **Identify the issue or argument.** In the example, the claim or conclusion is that the economy suffers when consumers cannot make rational decisions. Consumers cannot make rational decisions whenever information is lacking. The counterview is that consumer decision-making is based more on emotion than on rational reasoning. If that is the case, then information is not so important.

2. **Outline your ideas.** You are asked to take sides. If you believe that consumers make decisions mainly on a rational basis, you will have to support your view by giving examples based on experience or on the facts that you have acquired from study or reading. You must state why you support this view and not the other. Do you have any facts on the issue? If so, list them along with examples. If you do not have any facts, you will need to deal with the issue inferentially—by reasoning inductively. Here, experience and observation will be important to buttress your claims.

   Another possibility in this case is that consumer decision-making depends on the sort of product. When it comes to purchasing a house or making a similar capital investment, the decision is mainly rational, and so it depends on a good deal of information. Most consumer purchases, however, are not of this kind; for example, clothing, food, leisure activities—whose motivation is largely emotional. Thus, for most purchases, a lot of information is not necessary, and so the economy does not suffer as is claimed.

ANALYSIS OF AN ARGUMENT

The computerized water-irrigation system to be installed by farmers will prevent crops from drying out. The soil moisture is measured by sensors in the ground that send signals back to the irrigation control system. On the basis of this information, the system automatically regulates the amount and time of irrigation.

Discuss how logically persuasive you find this argument. In presenting your point of view, analyze the sort of reasoning used and its supporting evidence. In addition, state what further evidence, if any, would make the argument more sound and convincing or would make you better able to evaluate its conclusion.

TEST-TAKING TIPS

1. **Identify the parts of the argument.**
2. **State how convincing (or unconvincing) you find the argument.** The persuasiveness of an argument depends on its logic; that is, on whether the conclusion follows from the evidence presented. You are also asked to discuss what would make the argument more sound and persuasive or would help to evaluate its conclusion. To make an argument more sound, it is necessary to provide more evidence that will buttress the conclusion.

   In the example, the conclusion is found in the first sentence: the irrigation system wil prevent crops from drying out. What evidence is given that the irrigation system will indead perform its task? Overall, the argument is sound and convincing, assuming that proper irrigation is all that is needed to keep crops from drying out. What then could strengthen the conclusion? Evidence that systems similar to the one described are already in place and working. This last point is important because we have no evidence about the reliability of the system. Moreover, there may be a question of cost-effectiveness. Will farmers be willing to adopt such a system? If evidence of these factors could be provided, the conclusion would be strengthened.

Answer Sheet—Sample Test 1

Quantitative Section

1 Ⓐ Ⓑ Ⓒ Ⓓ Ⓔ	15 Ⓐ Ⓑ Ⓒ Ⓓ Ⓔ	29 Ⓐ Ⓑ Ⓒ Ⓓ Ⓔ
2 Ⓐ Ⓑ Ⓒ Ⓓ Ⓔ	16 Ⓐ Ⓑ Ⓒ Ⓓ Ⓔ	30 Ⓐ Ⓑ Ⓒ Ⓓ Ⓔ
3 Ⓐ Ⓑ Ⓒ Ⓓ Ⓔ	17 Ⓐ Ⓑ Ⓒ Ⓓ Ⓔ	31 Ⓐ Ⓑ Ⓒ Ⓓ Ⓔ
4 Ⓐ Ⓑ Ⓒ Ⓓ Ⓔ	18 Ⓐ Ⓑ Ⓒ Ⓓ Ⓔ	32 Ⓐ Ⓑ Ⓒ Ⓓ Ⓔ
5 Ⓐ Ⓑ Ⓒ Ⓓ Ⓔ	19 Ⓐ Ⓑ Ⓒ Ⓓ Ⓔ	33 Ⓐ Ⓑ Ⓒ Ⓓ Ⓔ
6 Ⓐ Ⓑ Ⓒ Ⓓ Ⓔ	20 Ⓐ Ⓑ Ⓒ Ⓓ Ⓔ	34 Ⓐ Ⓑ Ⓒ Ⓓ Ⓔ
7 Ⓐ Ⓑ Ⓒ Ⓓ Ⓔ	21 Ⓐ Ⓑ Ⓒ Ⓓ Ⓔ	35 Ⓐ Ⓑ Ⓒ Ⓓ Ⓔ
8 Ⓐ Ⓑ Ⓒ Ⓓ Ⓔ	22 Ⓐ Ⓑ Ⓒ Ⓓ Ⓔ	36 Ⓐ Ⓑ Ⓒ Ⓓ Ⓔ
9 Ⓐ Ⓑ Ⓒ Ⓓ Ⓔ	23 Ⓐ Ⓑ Ⓒ Ⓓ Ⓔ	37 Ⓐ Ⓑ Ⓒ Ⓓ Ⓔ
10 Ⓐ Ⓑ Ⓒ Ⓓ Ⓔ	24 Ⓐ Ⓑ Ⓒ Ⓓ Ⓔ	
11 Ⓐ Ⓑ Ⓒ Ⓓ Ⓔ	25 Ⓐ Ⓑ Ⓒ Ⓓ Ⓔ	
12 Ⓐ Ⓑ Ⓒ Ⓓ Ⓔ	26 Ⓐ Ⓑ Ⓒ Ⓓ Ⓔ	
13 Ⓐ Ⓑ Ⓒ Ⓓ Ⓔ	27 Ⓐ Ⓑ Ⓒ Ⓓ Ⓔ	
14 Ⓐ Ⓑ Ⓒ Ⓓ Ⓔ	28 Ⓐ Ⓑ Ⓒ Ⓓ Ⓔ	

Verbal Section

1 Ⓐ Ⓑ Ⓒ Ⓓ Ⓔ	15 Ⓐ Ⓑ Ⓒ Ⓓ Ⓔ	29 Ⓐ Ⓑ Ⓒ Ⓓ Ⓔ
2 Ⓐ Ⓑ Ⓒ Ⓓ Ⓔ	16 Ⓐ Ⓑ Ⓒ Ⓓ Ⓔ	30 Ⓐ Ⓑ Ⓒ Ⓓ Ⓔ
3 Ⓐ Ⓑ Ⓒ Ⓓ Ⓔ	17 Ⓐ Ⓑ Ⓒ Ⓓ Ⓔ	31 Ⓐ Ⓑ Ⓒ Ⓓ Ⓔ
4 Ⓐ Ⓑ Ⓒ Ⓓ Ⓔ	18 Ⓐ Ⓑ Ⓒ Ⓓ Ⓔ	32 Ⓐ Ⓑ Ⓒ Ⓓ Ⓔ
5 Ⓐ Ⓑ Ⓒ Ⓓ Ⓔ	19 Ⓐ Ⓑ Ⓒ Ⓓ Ⓔ	33 Ⓐ Ⓑ Ⓒ Ⓓ Ⓔ
6 Ⓐ Ⓑ Ⓒ Ⓓ Ⓔ	20 Ⓐ Ⓑ Ⓒ Ⓓ Ⓔ	34 Ⓐ Ⓑ Ⓒ Ⓓ Ⓔ
7 Ⓐ Ⓑ Ⓒ Ⓓ Ⓔ	21 Ⓐ Ⓑ Ⓒ Ⓓ Ⓔ	35 Ⓐ Ⓑ Ⓒ Ⓓ Ⓔ
8 Ⓐ Ⓑ Ⓒ Ⓓ Ⓔ	22 Ⓐ Ⓑ Ⓒ Ⓓ Ⓔ	36 Ⓐ Ⓑ Ⓒ Ⓓ Ⓔ
9 Ⓐ Ⓑ Ⓒ Ⓓ Ⓔ	23 Ⓐ Ⓑ Ⓒ Ⓓ Ⓔ	37 Ⓐ Ⓑ Ⓒ Ⓓ Ⓔ
10 Ⓐ Ⓑ Ⓒ Ⓓ Ⓔ	24 Ⓐ Ⓑ Ⓒ Ⓓ Ⓔ	38 Ⓐ Ⓑ Ⓒ Ⓓ Ⓔ
11 Ⓐ Ⓑ Ⓒ Ⓓ Ⓔ	25 Ⓐ Ⓑ Ⓒ Ⓓ Ⓔ	39 Ⓐ Ⓑ Ⓒ Ⓓ Ⓔ
12 Ⓐ Ⓑ Ⓒ Ⓓ Ⓔ	26 Ⓐ Ⓑ Ⓒ Ⓓ Ⓔ	40 Ⓐ Ⓑ Ⓒ Ⓓ Ⓔ
13 Ⓐ Ⓑ Ⓒ Ⓓ Ⓔ	27 Ⓐ Ⓑ Ⓒ Ⓓ Ⓔ	41 Ⓐ Ⓑ Ⓒ Ⓓ Ⓔ
14 Ⓐ Ⓑ Ⓒ Ⓓ Ⓔ	28 Ⓐ Ⓑ Ⓒ Ⓓ Ⓔ	

7

TWO SAMPLE GMATs WITH ANSWERS AND ANALYSIS

This chapter contains two full-length GMAT exams. They have the same formats and degrees of difficulty as typical GMAT exams. A detailed analysis of the answers is included after each.

SAMPLE TEST 1

WRITING ASSESSMENT

Part I   TIME: 30 MINUTES

> *Directions:* Write a clear, logical, and well-organized response to the following issue or argument. Your response should be in the form of a short essay, following the conventions of standard written English. Your answer should fit on three pages of lined 8½" × 11" paper or equivalent on your PC. Write legibly. Essays that are illegible or that are written on a topic other than the one outlined in the question will not be scored.

The fear is widespread among environmentalists that free trade increases economic growth and that growth harms the environment. That fear is misplaced. Growth enables governments to tax and to raise resources for a variety of objectives, including the abatement of pollution and the general protection of the environment. Without such revenues, little can be achieved, no matter how pure one's motives may be.

Which do you find more compelling, the fear of free trade or the response to it? Explain the position you take by using appropriate reasons, examples from your experience, reading, and study.

IF THERE IS STILL TIME REMAINING, YOU MAY REVIEW YOUR ANSWER. AFTER YOU HAVE CONFIRMED YOUR ANSWER, YOU CANNOT RETURN TO THIS QUESTION.

Part II   TIME: 30 MINUTES

> ***Directions:*** Write a clear, logical, and well-organized response to the following issue or argument. Your response should be in the form of a short essay, following the conventions of standard written English. Your answer should fit on three pages of lined 8½" × 11" paper or equivalent on your PC. Write legibly. Essays that are illegible or that are written on a topic other than the one outlined in the question will not be scored.

The installation of electronic high-speed scanning devices at the entrances and exits of toll roads will obviate the need for toll booths. Automobiles will have scanner-sensitive license plates— like the bar codes on consumer packaged products—so that the scanner devices will record the license numbers of cars entering and exiting the toll road. Car owners will be billed monthly by the highway authorities.

Discuss how logically persuasive you find the above argument. In presenting your point of view, analyze the sort of reasoning used and supporting evidence. In addition, state what further evidence, if any, would make the argument more sound and convincing or would make you better able to evaluate its conclusion.

> *IF THERE IS STILL TIME REMAINING, YOU MAY REVIEW YOUR ANSWER. AFTER YOU HAVE CONFIRMED YOUR ANSWER, YOU CANNOT RETURN TO THIS QUESTION.*

QUANTITATIVE SECTION

TIME: 75 MINUTES
37 QUESTIONS

This section consists of two types of questions: Problem Solving and
Data Sufficiency.

Problem Solving
Directions: Solve each of the following problems; then indicate the
correct answer.

NOTE: A figure that appears with a problem is drawn as accurately as
possible so as to provide information that may help in answering the
question.
Numbers in this test are real numbers.

Data Sufficiency
Directions: Each of the following problems has a question and two statements which are labeled (1) and (2). Use the data given in (1) and (2)
together with other available information (such as the number of hours in a
day, the definition of *clockwise*, mathematical facts, etc.) to decide whether
the statements are *sufficient* to answer the question. Then fill in space

(A) If you can get the answer from **(1) ALONE** but not from (2) alone
(B) If you can get the answer from **(2) ALONE** but not from (1) alone
(C) If you can get the answer from **BOTH (1) and (2) TOGETHER** but
    not from (1) alone or (2) alone
(D) If **EITHER** statement **(1) ALONE OR** statement **(2) ALONE** suffices
(E) If you **CANNOT** get the answer from statements (1) and (2)
    TOGETHER but need even more data

All numbers used in this section are real numbers.

A figure given for a problem is intended to provide information consis-
tent with that in the question, but not necessarily with the additional
information contained in the statements.
All figures lie in the plane unless you are told otherwise.
Figures are drawn as accurately as possible; straight lines may not
appear straight on the screen.

(A) If you can get the answer from **(1) ALONE** but not from (2) alone
(B) If you can get the answer from **(2) ALONE** but not from (1) alone
(C) If you can get the answer from **BOTH (1) and (2) TOGETHER** but not from (1) alone or (2) alone
(D) If **EITHER** statement **(1) ALONE OR** statement **(2) ALONE** suffices
(E) If you **CANNOT** get the answer from statements (1) and (2) **TOGETHER** but need even more data

1. It takes 30 days to fill a laboratory dish with bacteria. If the size of the bacteria colony doubles each day, how long did it take for the bacteria to fill one half of the dish?

   (A) 10 days
   (B) 15 days
   (C) 24 days
   (D) 29 days
   (E) 29.5 days

2. If the ratio of the areas of two squares is 2 : 1, then the ratio of the perimeters of the squares is

   (A) 1 : 2
   (B) 1 : $\sqrt{2}$
   (C) $\sqrt{2}$: 1
   (D) 2 : 1
   (E) 4 : 1

3. Are two triangles congruent?

   (1) Both triangles are right triangles.
   (2) Both triangles have the same perimeter.

4. Is x greater than zero?

   (1) $x^4 - 16 = 0$
   (2) $x^3 - 8 = 0$

(A) If you can get the answer from **(1) ALONE** but not from (2) alone
(B) If you can get the answer from **(2) ALONE** but not from (1) alone
(C) If you can get the answer from **BOTH (1) and (2) TOGETHER** but not from (1) alone or (2) alone
(D) If **EITHER** statement **(1) ALONE OR** statement **(2) ALONE** suffices
(E) If you **CANNOT** get the answer from statements (1) and (2) **TOGETHER** but need even more data

5. If both conveyer belt A and conveyer belt B are used, they can fill a hopper with coal in 1 hour. How long will it take for conveyer belt A to fill the hopper without conveyer belt B?

    (1) Conveyer belt A moves twice as much coal as conveyer belt B.
    (2) Conveyer belt B would take 3 hours to fill the hopper without conveyer belt A.

6. There are three types of tickets available for a concert: orchestra, which cost $12 each; balcony, which cost $9 each; and box, which cost $25 each. There were P orchestra tickets, B balcony tickets, and R box tickets sold for the concert. Which of the following expressions gives the percentage of ticket proceeds due to the sale of orchestra tickets?

    (A) $100 \times \dfrac{P}{(P + B + R)}$

    (B) $100 \times \dfrac{12P}{(12P + 9B + 25R)}$

    (C) $\dfrac{12P}{(12P + 9B + 25R)}$

    (D) $100 \times \dfrac{(9B + 25R)}{(12P + 9B + 25R)}$

    (E) $100 \times \dfrac{(12P + 9B + 25R)}{(12P)}$

(A) If you can get the answer from **(1) ALONE** but not from (2) alone

(B) If you can get the answer from **(2) ALONE** but not from (1) alone

(C) If you can get the answer from **BOTH (1) and (2) TOGETHER** but not from (1) alone or (2) alone

(D) If **EITHER** statement **(1) ALONE OR** statement **(2) ALONE** suffices

(E) If you **CANNOT** get the answer from statements (1) and (2) **TOGETHER** but need even more data

7. City B is 5 miles east of city A. City C is 10 miles southeast of city B. Which of the following is the closest to the distance from city A to city C?

   (A) 11 miles
   (B) 12 miles
   (C) 13 miles
   (D) 14 miles
   (E) 15 miles

8. There are 30 socks in a drawer. What is the probability that if 2 socks are picked from the drawer without looking both socks are blue?

   (1) 40 percent of the socks in the drawer are blue.
   (2) The ratio of blue socks to red socks in the drawer is 2 : 1.

9. If $3x - 2y = 8$, then $4y - 6x$ is

   (A) −16
   (B) −8
   (C) 8
   (D) 16
   (E) cannot be determined

10. It costs 10¢ a kilometer to fly and 12¢ a kilometer to drive. If you travel 200 kilometers, flying x kilometers of the distance and driving the rest, then the cost of the trip in dollars is

    (A) 20
    (B) 24
    (C) $24 - 2x$
    (D) $24 - .02x$
    (E) $2,400 - 2x$

(A) If you can get the answer from **(1) ALONE** but not from (2) alone

(B) If you can get the answer from **(2) ALONE** but not from (1) alone

(C) If you can get the answer from **BOTH (1) and (2) TOGETHER** but not from (1) alone or (2) alone

(D) If **EITHER** statement **(1) ALONE OR** statement **(2) ALONE** suffices

(E) If you **CANNOT** get the answer from statements (1) and (2) **TOGETHER** but need even more data

11. Is y larger than 1?

   (1) y is larger than 0.
   (2) $y^2 - 4 > 0$.

12. A worker is hired for 6 days. He is paid $2 more for each day of work than he was paid for the preceding day of work. How much was he paid for the first day of work?

   (1) His total wages for the 6 days were $150.
   (2) He was paid 150 percent of his first day's pay for the sixth day.

13. Let $^*y$ be the operation given by $^*y = \dfrac{4}{y} - y$. Which of the following statements are true?

   I. If $0 < y$, then $^*y$ is negative.
   II. If $0 < y < z$, then $^*y > {}^*z$.
   III. If $0 < y$ then $y(^*y)$ is less than 5.

   (A) I only
   (B) II only
   (C) III only
   (D) II and III
   (E) I, II, and III

14. A car originally sold for $3,000. After a month, the car was discounted x percent, and a month later the car's price was discounted y percent. Is the car's price after the discounts less than $2,600?

   (1) $y = 10$
   (2) $x = 15$

(A) If you can get the answer from **(1) ALONE** but not from (2) alone

(B) If you can get the answer from **(2) ALONE** but not from (1) alone

(C) If you can get the answer from **BOTH (1) and (2) TOGETHER** but not from (1) alone or (2) alone

(D) If **EITHER** statement **(1) ALONE OR** statement **(2) ALONE** suffices

(E) If you **CANNOT** get the answer from statements (1) and (2) **TOGETHER** but need even more data

15. How likely is a bird to be classified as positive?

    (1) 80 percent of birds with avian flu are classified as positive.
    (2) 5 percent of birds without avian flu are classified as positive.

16. If the area of a square increases by 69 percent, then the side of the square increases by

    (A) 13%
    (B) 30%
    (C) 39%
    (D) 69%
    (E) 130%

17. Which of the following statements can be inferred from the table?

Distribution of Work Hours in a Factory

Number of Workers		Number of Hours Worked
20		45–50
15		40–44
25		35–39
16		30–34
4		0–29
80	TOTAL	3,100

    I. The average number of hours worked per worker is less than 40.
    II. At least 3 workers worked more than 48 hours.
    III. More than half of all the workers worked more than 40 hours.

    (A) I only
    (B) II only
    (C) I and II only
    (D) I and III only
    (E) I, II, and III

18. When a truck travels at 60 miles per hour, it uses 30 percent more gasoline to travel any distance than it does when it travels at 50 miles per hour. The truck can travel 20 miles on a gallon of gas if it is traveling at 50 miles per hour. The truck has only 10 gallons of gas and is 160 miles from its destination. It takes 20 minutes for the truck to stop for gas. How long will it take the truck to reach its final destination if it is driven at 60 miles per hour?

   (A) 160 minutes
   (B) 180 minutes
   (C) 190 minutes
   (D) 192 minutes
   (E) 195 minutes

19. Company *A* owns 40 percent of the stock in the XYZ Corporation. Company *B* owns 15,000 shares. Company *C* owns all the shares not owned by company *A* or *B*. How many shares of stock does company *A* own if company *C* has 25 percent more shares than company *A*?

   (A) 45,000
   (B) 50,000
   (C) 60,000
   (D) 75,000
   (E) 90,000

20. How many squares with sides $\frac{1}{2}$ inch long are needed to cover a rectangle that is 4 feet long and 6 feet wide?

   (A) 24
   (B) 96
   (C) 3,456
   (D) 13,824
   (E) 14,266

(A) If you can get the answer from **(1) ALONE** but not from (2) alone
(B) If you can get the answer from **(2) ALONE** but not from (1) alone
(C) If you can get the answer from **BOTH (1) and (2) TOGETHER** but not from (1) alone or (2) alone
(D) If **EITHER** statement **(1) ALONE OR** statement **(2) ALONE** suffices
(E) If you **CANNOT** get the answer from statements (1) and (2) **TOGETHER** but need even more data

21. How much cardboard will it take to make an open cubical box with no top?

   (1) The area of the bottom of the box is 4 square feet.
   (2) The volume of the box is 8 cubic feet.

22. Is the integer x divisible by 3?

   (1) The last digit in x is 3.
   (2) $x + 5$ is divisible by 6.

23. Is the figure $ABCD$ a rectangle?

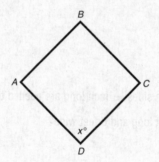

   (1) $x = 90$
   (2) $AB = CD$

(A) If you can get the answer from **(1) ALONE** but not from (2) alone

(B) If you can get the answer from **(2) ALONE** but not from (1) alone

(C) If you can get the answer from **BOTH (1) and (2) TOGETHER** but not from (1) alone or (2) alone

(D) If **EITHER** statement **(1) ALONE OR** statement **(2) ALONE** suffices

(E) If you **CANNOT** get the answer from statements (1) and (2) **TOGETHER** but need even more data

24. A sequence of numbers is given by the rule $a_n = (a_{n-1})^2$. What is a_5?

    (1) $a_1 = -1$

    (2) $a_3 = 1$

25. In a group of people solicited by a charity, 30 percent contributed $40 each, 45 percent contributed $20 each, and the rest contributed $12 each. What percentage of the total contributed came from people who gave $40?

    (A) 25%

    (B) 30%

    (C) 40%

    (D) 45%

    (E) 50%

26. A trapezoid *ABCD* is formed by adding the isosceles right triangle *BCE* with base 5 inches to the rectangle *ABED*, where *DE* is *t* inches. What is the area of the trapezoid in square inches?

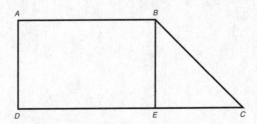

    (A) $5t + 12.5$

    (B) $5t + 25$

    (C) $2.5t + 12.5$

    (D) $(t + 5)^2$

    (E) $t^2 + 25$

27. A manufacturer of jam wants to make a profit of $75 when it sells 300 jars of jam. It costs 65¢ each to make the first 100 jars of jam and 55¢ each to make each jar after the first 100. What price should it charge for the 300 jars of jam?

    (A) $75
    (B) $175
    (C) $225
    (D) $240
    (E) $250

28. A car traveled 75 percent of the distance from town A to town B by traveling for T hours at an average speed of V miles per hour. The car traveled at an average speed of S miles per hour for the remaining part of the trip. Which of the following expressions represents the time the car traveled at S miles per hour?

    (A) $\dfrac{VT}{S}$

    (B) $\dfrac{VS}{4T}$

    (C) $\dfrac{4VT}{3S}$

    (D) $\dfrac{3S}{VT}$

    (E) $\dfrac{VT}{3S}$

(A) If you can get the answer from **(1) ALONE** but not from (2) alone

(B) If you can get the answer from **(2) ALONE** but not from (1) alone

(C) If you can get the answer from **BOTH (1) and (2) TOGETHER** but not from (1) alone or (2) alone

(D) If **EITHER** statement **(1) ALONE OR** statement **(2) ALONE** suffices

(E) If you **CANNOT** get the answer from statements (1) and (2) **TOGETHER** but need even more data

29. How much is John's weekly salary?

   (1) John's weekly salary is twice as much as Fred's weekly salary.
   (2) Fred's weekly salary is 40 percent of the total of Chuck's weekly salary and John's weekly salary.

30. Find $x + 2y$.

   (1) $x + y = 4$
   (2) $2x + 4y = 12$

31. Is angle BAC a right angle?

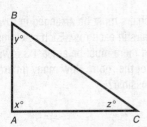

   (1) $x = 2y$
   (2) $y = 1.5z$

(A) If you can get the answer from **(1) ALONE** but not from (2) alone

(B) If you can get the answer from **(2) ALONE** but not from (1) alone

(C) If you can get the answer from **BOTH (1) and (2) TOGETHER** but not from (1) alone or (2) alone

(D) If **EITHER** statement **(1) ALONE OR** statement **(2) ALONE** suffices

(E) If you **CANNOT** get the answer from statements (1) and (2) **TOGETHER** but need even more data

32. If a, b, and c are digits, is $a + b + c$ a multiple of 9? A digit is one of the integers 0, 1, 2, 3, 4, 5, 6, 7, 8, 9.

    (1) The three-digit number abc is a multiple of 9.
    (2) $(a \times b) + c$ is a multiple of 9.

33. In Teetown 50 percent of the people have blue eyes and blond hair. What percent of the people in Teetown have blue eyes but do not have blond hair?

    (1) 70 percent of the people in Teetown have blond hair.
    (2) 60 percent of the people in Teetown have blue eyes.

34. Thirty-six identical chairs must be arranged in rows with the same number of chairs in each row. Each row must contain at least 3 chairs, and there must be at least 3 rows. A row is parallel to the front of the room. How many different arrangements are possible?

    (A) 2
    (B) 4
    (C) 5
    (D) 6
    (E) 10

35. Which of the following solids has the largest volume? (*Figures are not drawn to scale.*)

I. A cylinder of radius 5 millimeters and height 11 millimeters

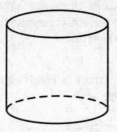

II. A sphere of radius 6 millimeters (the volume of a sphere of radius r is $\frac{4}{3}\pi r^3$)

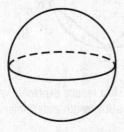

III. A cube with edge of 9 millimeters.

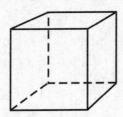

(A) I
(B) II
(C) III
(D) I and II
(E) II and III

(A) If you can get the answer from **(1) ALONE** but not from (2) alone

(B) If you can get the answer from **(2) ALONE** but not from (1) alone

(C) If you can get the answer from **BOTH (1) and (2) TOGETHER** but not from (1) alone or (2) alone

(D) If **EITHER** statement **(1) ALONE OR** statement **(2) ALONE** suffices

(E) If you **CANNOT** get the answer from statements (1) and (2) **TOGETHER** but need even more data

36. The pentagon *ABCDE* is inscribed in a circle with center *O*. How many degrees is angle *ABC*?

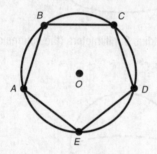

   (1) The pentagon *ABCDE* is a regular pentagon, which means that all sides are the same length and all interior angles are the same size.
   (2) The radius of the circle is 5 inches.

37. Is $k^2 + k - 2 > 0$?

   (1) $k < 1$
   (2) $k > -1$

IF THERE IS STILL TIME REMAINING, YOU MAY REVIEW YOUR ANSWER. AFTER YOU HAVE CONFIRMED YOUR ANSWER, YOU CANNOT RETURN TO THIS QUESTION.

VERBAL SECTION

TIME: 75 MINUTES
41 QUESTIONS

Reading Comprehension
Directions: This section contains three reading passages. You are to read each one carefully. When answering the questions, you *will* be allowed to refer back to the passages. The questions are based on what is *stated* or *implied* in each passage.

Critical Reasoning
Directions: For each question in this section, choose the best answer among the listed alternatives.

Sentence Correction
Directions: This part of the section consists of a number of sentences in each of which some part or the whole is underlined. Each sentence is followed by five alternative versions of the underlined portion. Select the alternative you consider both most correct and most effective according to the requirements of standard written English. Answer (A) is the same as the original version; if you think the original version is best, select answer (A).

In considering the answer choices, be attentive to matters of grammar, diction, and syntax, as well as clarity, precision, and fluency. Do not select an answer that alters the meaning of the original sentence.

1. Farmers in the North have observed that heavy frost is usually preceded by a full moon. They are convinced that the full moon somehow generates the frost.

   Which of the following, if true, would weaken the farmers' conviction?

   (A) The temperature must fall below 10 degrees Celsius (50 degrees Fahrenheit) for frost to occur.
   (B) Absence of a cloud cover cools the ground which causes frost.
   (C) Farmers are superstitious.
   (D) No one has proven that the moon causes frost.
   (E) Farmers are not experts in meteorology.

2. Professor Tembel told his class that the method of student evaluation of teachers is not a valid measure of teaching quality. Students should fill out questionnaires at the end of the semester when courses have been completed.

   Which of the following, if true, provides support for Professor Tembel's proposal?

   (A) Professor Tembel received low ratings from his students.
   (B) Students filled out questionnaires after the midterm exam.
   (C) Students are interested in teacher evaluation.
   (D) Teachers are not obligated to use the survey results.
   (E) Student evaluation of teachers is voluntary.

3. If she was to decide to go to college, I, for one, would recommend that she plan to go to Yale.

   (A) If she was to decide to go to college,
   (B) If she were to decide to go to college,
   (C) Had she decided to go to college,
   (D) In the event that she decides to go to college,
   (E) Supposing she was to decide to go to college,

4. <u>Except for you and I, everyone brought</u> a present to the party.

   (A) Except for you and I, everyone brought
   (B) With exception of you and I, everyone brought
   (C) Except for you and I, everyone had brought
   (D) Except for you and me, everyone brought
   (E) Except for you and me, everyone had brought

Questions 5–8 are based on the following passage.

The domestic economy expanded in a remarkably vigorous and steady fashion. . . . The resurgence in consumer confidence was reflected in the higher proportion of incomes spent for goods and services and the marked increase in consumer willingness to take
(5) on installment debt. A parallel strengthening in business psychology was manifested in a stepped-up rate of plant and equipment spending and a gradual pickup in outlays for inventory. Confidence in the economy was also reflected in the strength of the stock market and in the stability of the bond market. . . . For the year as a
(10) whole, consumer and business sentiment benefited from rising public expectations that a resolution of the conflict in Vietnam was in prospect and that East-West tensions were easing.

The United States balance of payments deficit declined sharply. Nevertheless, by any other test, the deficit remained very large, and
(15) there was actually a substantial deterioration in our trade account to a sizable deficit, almost two thirds of which was with Japan. . . .

The underlying task of public policy for the year ahead—and indeed for the longer run—remained a familiar one: to strike the right balance between encouraging healthy economic growth and
(20) avoiding inflationary pressures. With the economy showing sustained and vigorous growth, and with the currency crisis highlighting the need to improve our competitive posture internationally, the emphasis seemed to be shifting to the problem of inflation. The Phase Three program of wage and price restraint can contribute to
(25) dampening inflation. Unless productivity growth is unexpectedly large, however, the expansion of real output must eventually begin to slow down to the economy's larger run growth potential if generalized demand pressures on prices are to be avoided. Indeed, while the unemployment rates of a bit over five percent were still
(30) too high, it seems doubtful whether the much lower rates of four percent and below often cited as appropriate definitions of full employment do in fact represent feasible goals for the United

States economy—unless there are improvements in the structure of labor and product markets and public policies influencing their
(35) operation. There is little doubt that overall unemployment rates can be brought down to four percent or less, for a time at least, by sufficient stimulation of aggregate demand. However, the resultant inflationary pressures have in the past proved exceedingly difficult to contain.

5. The passage was most likely published in a

   (A) popular magazine
   (B) general newspaper
   (C) science journal
   (D) financial journal
   (E) textbook

6. Confidence in the economy was expressed by all of the following except

   (A) a strong stock market
   (B) a stable bond market
   (C) increased installment debt
   (D) increased plant and equipment expenditures
   (E) rising interest rates

7. According to the passage, a major problem is how to

   (A) sustain economic growth
   (B) improve labor productivity
   (C) balance growth with low inflation
   (D) stimulate demand
   (E) avoid large increases in imports

8. Most of the trade deficit in the balance of payments was attributed to trade with which country?

   (A) United Kingdom
   (B) Japan
   (C) Germany
   (D) France
   (E) Saudi Arabia

9. When one reads the poetry of the seventeenth century, you find a striking contrast between the philosophy of the Cavalier poets such as Suckling and the attitude of the Metaphysical poets such as Donne.

   (A) When one reads the poetry of the seventeenth century, you find
   (B) When you read the poetry of the seventeenth century, one finds
   (C) When one reads the poetry of the seventeenth century, he finds
   (D) If one reads the poetry of the 17th century, you find
   (E) As you read the poetry of the 17th century, one finds

10. Because of his broken hip, John Jones has not and possibly never will be able to run the mile again.

    (A) has not and possibly never will be able to run
    (B) has not and possibly will never be able to run
    (C) has not been and possibly never would be able to run
    (D) has not and possibly never would be able to run
    (E) has not been able to run and possibly never will be able to run

11. The President lobbied for passage of his new trade bill which would liberalize trade with industrialized countries such as Japan, members of the European Community, and Canada.

    Each of the following, if true, could account for the above, except:

    (A) The President is up for re-election and needs to show results.
    (B) Labor unions have petitioned the President to provide more local jobs.
    (C) The trade agreement could bring a *quid pro quo* on pending negotiations.
    (D) Economists claimed that the passage of the bill would increase the country's trade deficit.
    (E) It was politically desirable for a trade bill at the present time.

12. If we are doomed to have local drug rehabilitation centers—
    and society has determined that we are—then society ought to
    pay for them.

    Which of the following, if true, would weaken the above argument?

    (A) Drug rehabilitation centers are too expensive to be locally
        funded.
    (B) Many neighborhood groups oppose rehabilitation centers.
    (C) Drug rehabilitation centers are expensive to maintain.
    (D) Drug addicts may be unwilling to receive treatment.
    (E) A government committee has convinced many groups that
        local rehabilitation centers are ineffective.

Questions 13–16 are based on the following passage.

These huge waves wreak terrific damage when they crash on the
shores of distant lands or continents. Under a perfectly sunny sky
and from an apparently calm sea, a wall of water may break twenty
or thirty feet high over beaches and waterfronts, crushing houses
(5) and drowning unsuspecting residents and bathers in its path.

How are these waves formed? When a submarine earthquake
occurs, it is likely to set up a tremendous amount of shock, dis-
turbing the quiet waters of the deep ocean. This disturbance travels to the surface and forms a huge swell in the ocean many miles
(10) across. It rolls outward in all directions, and the water lowers in the
center as another swell looms up. Thus, a series of concentric
swells are formed similar to those made when a coin or small peb-
ble is dropped into a basin of water. The big difference is in the size.
Each of the concentric rings of basin water traveling out toward the
(15) edge is only about an inch across and less than a quarter of an inch
high. The swells in the ocean are sometimes nearly a mile wide and
rise to several multiples of ten feet in height.

Many of us have heard about these waves, often referred to by
their Japanese name of "tsunami." For ages they have been
(20) dreaded in the Pacific, as no shore has been free from them. An
underwater earthquake in the Aleutian Islands could start a swell
that would break along the shores and cause severe damage in the
southern part of Chile in South America. These waves travel hundreds of miles an hour, and one can understand how they would
(25) crash as violent breakers when caused to drag in the shallow
waters of a coast.

Nothing was done about tsunamis until after World War II. In 1947 a particularly bad submarine earthquake took place south of the Aleutian Islands. A few hours later, people bathing in the sun
(30) along the quiet shores of Hawaii were dashed to death and shoreline property became a mass of shambles because a series of monstrous, breaking swells crashed along the shore and drove far inland. Hundreds of lives were lost in this catastrophe, and millions upon millions of dollars' worth of damage was done.

13. One surprising aspect of the waves discussed in the passage is the fact that they

   (A) are formed in concentric patterns
   (B) often strike during clear weather
   (C) arise under conditions of cold temperature
   (D) are produced by deep swells
   (E) may be forecast scientifically

14. The waves discussed in the passage often strike

   (A) along the coasts of the Aleutian Islands
   (B) in regions outside the area monitored by the Coast and Geodetic Survey
   (C) at great distances from their place of origin
   (D) at the same time as the occurrence of earthquakes
   (E) in areas outside the Pacific region

15. It is believed that the waves are caused by

   (A) seismic changes
   (B) concentric time belts
   (C) atmospheric conditions
   (D) underwater earthquakes
   (E) storms

16. A possible title for the passage could be

   (A) How Submarine Waves Are Formed
   (B) How to Locate Submarine Earthquakes
   (C) Underwater Earthquakes
   (D) "Tsunami" Waves
   (E) How to Prevent Submarine Earthquakes

17. <u>Had I realized how close</u> I was to failing, I would not have gone to the party.

   (A) Had I realized how close
   (B) If I would have realized
   (C) Had I had realized how close
   (D) When I realized how close
   (E) If I realized how close

18. <u>The football team's winning it's first game of the season</u> excited the student body.

   (A) The football team's winning it's first game of the season
   (B) The football team having won it's first game of the season
   (C) The football team's having won it's first game of the season
   (D) The football team's winning its first game of the season
   (E) The football team winning it's first game of the season

19. Anyone interested in the use of computers can learn much <u>if you have access to</u> a state-of-the-art microcomputer.

   (A) if you have access to
   (B) if he has access to
   (C) if access is available to
   (D) by access to
   (E) from access to

20. <u>No student had ought to be put into a situation where</u> he has to choose between his loyalty to his friends and his duty to the class.

   (A) No student had ought to be put into a situation where
   (B) No student had ought to be put into a situation in which
   (C) No student should be put into a situation where
   (D) No student ought to be put into a situation in which
   (E) No student ought to be put into a situation where

21. <u>Being a realist,</u> I could not accept her statement that supernatural beings had caused the disturbance.

    (A) Being a realist,
    (B) Since I am a realist,
    (C) Being that I am a realist,
    (D) Being as I am a realist,
    (E) Realist that I am,

22. Surviving this crisis is going to take everything we've got. In addition to … massive retraining, we may also need subsidies—direct or channeled through the private sector—for a radically expanding service sector. Not merely things like environmental clean-up, but basic human services. (Alvin Toffler, *Previews and Premises* (New York: Bantam Books, 1985), p. 57.)

    Which of the following statements is inconsistent with the above?

    (A) Subsidies are needed to overcome the crisis.
    (B) Environmental controls will be loosened.
    (C) The service sector is going to expand to such an extent that many more workers will be needed.
    (D) The private sector will play a role in retraining workers.
    (E) Before the crisis can end, an environmental clean-up will have to take place.

23. Per-capita income last year was $25,000. Per-capita income is calculated by dividing total aggregate cash income by the total population. Real median income for families headed by a female, with no husband present, was $29,000. Therefore, women wage-earners earned more than the national average.

    Which of the following would, if true, weaken the above conclusion?

    (A) Per-capita income is calculated in real terms.
    (B) In 99 percent of the cases, families headed by a female included no other wage-earner.
    (C) Average income is not significantly different from median income.
    (D) The overall average and per-capita income were the same.
    (E) Only a small proportion of the total wage earners are women family heads.

Questions 24–27 are based on the following passage.

I decided to begin the term's work with the short story since that form would be the easiest for [the police officers], not only because most of their reading up to then had probably been in that genre, but also because a study of the reaction of people to various situa-
(5) tions was something they relied on in their daily work.

The officer must remain neutral and clearly try to present a pic-ture of the facts, while the artist usually begins with a preconceived message or attitude which is then transmitted through the use of carefully selected details of action described in words intended to
(10) provoke associations and emotional reactions in the reader. Only at the end of the term did the officer point out to me that he and his men also try to evaluate the events they describe and that their description of a sequence of events must of necessity be structured and colored by their understanding of what has taken place.

(15) The policemen's reactions to events and characters in the sto-ries were surprisingly unprejudiced . . . . They did not object to writ-ers whose stories had to do with their protagonist's rebellion against society's accepted values. Nor did stories in which the strong father becomes the villain and in which our usual ideals of
(20) manhood are turned around offend them. The many hunters among my students readily granted the message in those hunting tales in which sensitivity triumphs over male aggressiveness, stories that show the boy becoming a man because he fails to shoot the deer, goose, or catbird. The only characters they did object to were those
(25) they thought unrealistic. As the previous class had done, this one also excelled in interpreting the ways in which characters reveal themselves, subtly manipulate and influence each other; they, too, understood how the story usually saves its insight, its revelation, for the end.

(30) This almost instinctive grasp of the writing of fiction was revealed when the policemen volunteered to write their own short stories. . . . They not only took great pains with plot and character, but with style and language. The stories were surprisingly well writ-ten, revealing an understanding of what a solid short story must
(35) contain: the revelation of character, the use of background descrip-tion and language to create atmosphere and mood, the need to sus-tain suspense and yet make each event as it occurs seem natural, the insight achieved either by the characters in the story or the reader or both. They tended to favor surprise endings. Some sto-

(40) ries were sheer fantasies, or derived from previous reading, films, or television shows. Most wrote stories, obviously based on their own experiences, that revealed the amazing distance they must put between their personal lives and their work. These stories demonstrated how clearly, almost naively, these policemen wanted to con-
(45) tinue to believe in some of the so-called American virtues—that courage is worth the effort and will be admired; that hard work will be rewarded; that life is somehow good; and that, despite the weariness, boredom, and occasional ugliness and danger, despite all their dislike of most of their routine and despite their own occa-
(50) sional grousing and complaints, they somehow did like being cops; that life, even in a chaotic and violent world, is worth it after all.

24. Compared to the artist, the policeman is

   (A) ruled by action, not words
   (B) factual and not fanciful
   (C) neutral and not prejudiced
   (D) stoic and not emotional
   (E) aggressive and not passive

25. Policemen reacted to story events and characters

   (A) like most other people
   (B) according to a policeman's stereotyped image
   (C) like dilettantes
   (D) unrealistically
   (E) without emotion

26. To which sort of characters did policemen object?

    I. Unrealistic
   II. Emotional
   III. Sordid

   (A) I only
   (B) II only
   (C) I and II only
   (D) II and III only
   (E) I, II, and III

27. The instructor chose the short story because

    I. it was easy for the students
    II. students had experience with it
    III. students would enjoy it

    (A) I only
    (B) II only
    (C) I and II only
    (D) II and III only
    (E) I, II, and III

28. Foreign investment is composed of direct investment transactions (investment in plant, equipment and land) and securities investment transactions. Throughout the post-World War II period, net increases in U.S. direct investment in Europe (funds outflows) exceeded net new European direct investment in the U.S.

    Each of the following, if true, could help to account for this trend except:

    (A) Land values in Europe were increasing at a faster rate than in the United States.
    (B) Duties on imported goods in Europe were higher than those imposed by the United States.
    (C) The cost of labor (wages) was consistently lower in Europe than in the United States.
    (D) Labor mobility was much higher in the United States than in Europe.
    (E) Corporate liquidity was lower in Europe than in the United States.

29. Most large retail stores hold sales in the month of January. The original idea of price reduction campaigns in January became popular when it was realized that sales of products would generally slow down following the Christmas rush, were it not for some incentive. The lack of demand could be solved by the simple solution of reducing prices.

    There is now an increasing tendency among major department stores in large urban centers to have their "January sales" begin before Christmas, some time before the end of the calendar year. The idea behind this trend is to endeavor to sell the maximum amount of stock at a profit, even if that may not be at the maximum profit.

    Which of the following conclusions cannot be drawn from the above?

    (A) The incidence of "early" January sales results in the lower holdings of stocks with the corollary of lower stock holding costs.
    (B) Demand is a function of price; as you lower price, demand increases.
    (C) Major stores seem to think it makes sense to have the January sales campaigns pre-Christmas.
    (D) It is becoming less popular to start the January sales in the New Year.
    (E) The major department stores do not worry as much about profit maximization as they do about sales maximization.

30. The reason I came late to class today is because the bus broke down.

    (A) I came late to class today is because
    (B) why I came late to class today is because
    (C) I was late to school today is because
    (D) that I was late to school today is because
    (E) I came late to class today is that

31. The grocer <u>hadn't hardly any of those kind</u> of canned goods.

    (A) hadn't hardly any of those kind
    (B) hadn't hardly any of those kinds
    (C) had hardly any of those kind
    (D) had hardly any of those kinds
    (E) had scarcely any of those kind

32. <u>Having stole the money, the police searched the thief.</u>

    (A) Having stole the money, the police searched the thief.
    (B) Having stolen the money, the thief was searched by the police.
    (C) Having stolen the money, the police searched the thief.
    (D) Having stole the money, the thief was searched by the police.
    (E) Being that he stole the money, the police searched the thief.

33. The child is <u>neither encouraged to be critical or to examine</u> all the evidence for his opinion.

    (A) neither encouraged to be critical or to examine
    (B) neither encouraged to be critical nor to examine
    (C) either encouraged to be critical or to examine
    (D) encouraged either to be critical nor to examine
    (E) not encouraged either to be critical or to examine

34. The process by which the community <u>influence the actions of its members</u> is known as social control.

    (A) influence the actions of its members
    (B) influences the actions of its members
    (C) had influenced the actions of its members
    (D) influences the actions of their members
    (E) will influence the actions of its members

35. Of the world's largest external-debt countries in 1999, three had the same share of world external-debt as they had in 1990. These three countries may serve as examples of countries that succeeded in holding steady their share of world external-debt.

    Which of the following, if true, would most seriously undermine the idea that these countries serve as examples as described above?

    (A) Of the three countries, two had a much larger share of world external-debt in 1995 than in 1999.
    (B) Some countries strive to reduce their share of world external-debt, not keep it steady.
    (C) The three countries have different rates of economic growth.
    (D) The absolute value of debt of the three countries is different.
    (E) Some countries are more concerned with internal budgets than with external debt.

36. The director of the customs service suggested that customs taxes on automobiles not be reduced as planned by the government because of the high incidence of traffic accidents last year.

    Which of the above statements weakens the argument above?

    I. Although the traffic accident rate last year was high, it was not appreciably higher than previous years and anyway, compulsory insurance covered most physical damage to automobiles and property.
    II. A Commerce Department report showed that the demand for automobiles was highly inelastic. That is, as dealers lowered their prices, sales did not increase appreciably.
    III. A study by the Economics Department at Classics University found that most traffic accidents had been caused by human error although it also concluded that an inadequate road network contributed to at least 40 percent of passenger injuries.

    (A) I, but not II and not III.
    (B) II, but not I and not III.
    (C) I and III, but not II.
    (D) II and III, but not I.
    (E) I, II and III.

37. Significant beneficial effects of smoking occur primarily in the area of mental health, and the habit originates in a search for contentment. The life expectancy of our people has increased greatly in recent years; it is possible that the relaxation and contentment and enjoyment produced by smoking has lengthened many lives. Smoking is beneficial.

Which of the following, if true, weaken the above conclusion?

(A) That cigarettes are a major health hazard cannot be traced to the willfull act of any human or organization.
(B) The government earns millions of dollars from the tobacco tax and tens of thousands of civilians are employed in the tobacco industry.
(C) The evidence cited in the statement covers only one example of the effects of cigarette smoking.
(D) No mention is made of possible harmful side-effects of smoking.
(E) No statistical evidence has proven a link between smoking and longevity.

38. An economist was quoted as saying that the Consumer Price Index (CPI) will go up next month because of a recent increase in the price of fruit and vegetables.

Which of the following cannot be inferred from the statement?

(A) The cost of fruits and vegetables has risen sharply.
(B) Consumers have decreased their consumption of fruits and vegetables.
(C) The cost of fruit and vegetables is a major item in the CPI.
(D) Food cost changes are reflected quickly in the CPI.
(E) Other items that make up the CPI have not significantly decreased in price.

39. At a political rally at Jefferson Stadium, candidate Smith exclaimed: "Nearly everyone at the rally is behind me. It looks like I am going to be elected."

   Which of the following statements, if true, best supports the above conclusion?

   (A) Smith's opponent also appeared at the rally.
   (B) The rally was attended by almost all the residents of Smith's constituency.
   (C) Smith was never defeated in an election.
   (D) Smith was supported by the local mayor.
   (E) People always vote their emotions.

40. Depending on skillful suggestion, argument is seldom used in advertising.

   (A) Depending on skillful suggestion, argument is seldom used in advertising.
   (B) Argument is seldom used by advertisers, who depend instead on skillful suggestion.
   (C) Skillfull suggestion is depended on by advertisers instead of argument.
   (D) Suggestion, which is more skillful, is used in place of argument by advertisers.
   (E) Instead of suggestion, depending on argument is used by skillful advertisers.

41. In a famous experiment by Pavlov, when a dog smelled food, it salivated. Subsequently, a bell was rung whenever food was placed near the dog. After a number of trials, only the bell was rung, whereupon the dog would salivate even though no food was present.

Which of the following conclusions may be drawn from the above experiment?

(A) Dogs are easily fooled.
(B) Dogs are motivated only by the sound of a bell.
(C) The ringing of a bell was associated with food.
(D) A conclusion cannot be reached on the basis of one experiment.
(E) Two stimuli are stronger than one.

IF THERE IS STILL TIME REMAINING, YOU MAY REVIEW YOUR ANSWER. AFTER YOU HAVE CONFIRMED YOUR ANSWER, YOU CANNOT RETURN TO THIS QUESTION.

ANSWER KEY

SAMPLE TEST 1

Quantitative Section

1. D	11. C	21. D	31. C
2. C	12. D	22. B	32. A
3. E	13. D	23. E	33. B
4. B	14. B	24. D	34. C
5. D	15. E	25. E	35. B
6. B	16. B	26. A	36. A
7. D	17. A	27. E	37. C
8. A	18. B	28. E	
9. A	19. C	29. E	
10. D	20. D	30. B	

Verbal Section

1. B	12. E	23. E	34. B
2. B	13. B	24. C	35. A
3. B	14. C	25. A	36. B
4. D	15. D	26. A	37. E
5. D	16. A	27. C	38. B
6. E	17. A	28. D	39. B
7. C	18. D	29. A	40. B
8. B	19. B	30. E	41. C
9. C	20. D	31. D	
10. E	21. A	32. B	
11. D	22. B	33. E	

ANALYSIS

Self-Scoring Guide—Analytical Writing

Evaluate your writing tests (or have a friend or teacher evaluate them for you) on the following basis. Read each essay completely, paying special attention to its logical organization and use of examples and facts to buttress its claims or position. Assign a holistic score between 0 and 6, using the scale below. Your writing score will be the average of the scores of the two essays.

6   **Outstanding:** Cogent, well-articulated analysis of the issue or critique of the argument. Develops a position with insightful reasons and persuasive examples. Well organized. Superior command of language and variety of syntax. Only minor flaws in grammar, usage, and mechanics.

5   **Strong:** Well-developed analysis or critique. Develops a position with well-chosen examples or reasons. Generally well organized. Clear control of language and variety of syntax. Minor flaws in grammar, usage, and mechanics.

4   **Adequate:** Competent analysis or critique. Develops a position with relevant reasons or examples. Adequately organized. Adequate control of language, but may lack syntactic variety. May have some flaws in grammar, usage, and mechanics.

3   **Limited:** Competent but clearly flawed analysis or critique. Vague or limited in developing a position. Poorly organized. Weak in using relevant examples or reasons. Language used imprecisely or lacking in sentence variety. Contains major errors or frequent minor errors in grammar, usage, and mechanics.

2   **Seriously Flawed:** Serious weaknesses in analysis and organization. Unclear or seriously limited in presenting or developing a position. Disorganized. Few relevant examples or reasons. Frequent serious problems in language and sentence structure. Numerous errors in grammar, usage, or mechanics that interfere with meaning.

1   **Fundamentally Deficient:** Little evidence of ability to organize and develop a coherent response to issue or argument. Severe and persistent errors in language and sentence structure. Pervasive pattern of errors in grammar, usage, and mechanics that severely interfere with meaning.

0   **Unscorable:** Illegible or not written in the assigned topic.

ANSWERS EXPLAINED

Quantitative Section

1. **(D)**

Difficulty Level

Since the size of the bacteria colony doubles each day, the dish must be half full 1 day before it is full. So the correct answer is 29 days, or choice (D). A common mistake is to choose (B), but that gives half the time it takes to fill the dish, not the time when the dish is half full. If the question had asked when the dish was one-quarter full, the correct answer would be 28 days.

2. **(C)**

Difficulty Level

If s and t denote the sides of the two squares, then $s^2 : t^2 = 2 : 1$.

Thus, $\left(\dfrac{s}{t}\right)^2 = \dfrac{2}{1}$ and $\dfrac{s}{t} = \dfrac{\sqrt{2}}{1}$. Since the ratio of the perimeters is

$4s : 4t = s : t$, (C) is the correct answer.

3. **(E)**

Difficulty Level

A triangle with sides of lengths 3, 4, and 5 is a right triangle since $3^2 + 4^2 = 5^2$, and its perimeter is 12. A triangle with sides of lengths 2, 4.8, and 5.2 also has a perimeter of 12. And since $2^2 + (4.8)^2 = (5.2)^2$, it too is a right triangle. Therefore, two triangles can satisfy STATEMENTS (1) and (2) yet not be congruent. On the other hand, any pair of congruent right triangles satisfy STATEMENTS (1) and (2). Thus, STATEMENTS (1) and (2) together are not sufficient to answer the question.

4. **(B)**

Difficulty Level

$x^3 - 8 = 0$ has only $x = 2$ as a real solution. And 2 is greater than 0, so STATEMENT (2) alone is sufficient.

Since $x = 2$ and $x = -2$ are both solutions of $x^4 - 16 = 0$, STATEMENT (1) alone is not sufficient.

5. **(D)**

⑤

Difficulty Level

STATEMENT (1) is sufficient since it implies that conveyer belt A loads $\frac{2}{3}$ of the hopper while conveyer belt B loads only $\frac{1}{3}$ with both working. Since conveyer belt A loads $\frac{2}{3}$ of the hopper in a hour, it will take $1 \div \left(\frac{2}{3}\right)$ or 1.5 hours to fill the hopper by itself.

STATEMENT (2) is also sufficient since it implies that conveyer belt B fills $\frac{1}{3}$ of the hopper in 1 hour. Thus, conveyer belt A loads $\frac{2}{3}$ in 1 hour, and that means conveyer belt A would take 1.5 hours by itself.

6. **(B)**

⑧

Difficulty Level

First find an expression for the proceeds from orchestra tickets, which is $12P$. Next, find an expression for the total proceeds, which is $12P + 9B + 25R$. So $\frac{12P}{(12P + 9B + 25R)}$ gives the part of the total proceeds due to the sale of orchestra tickets. However, this is not a percentage. You need to multiply this expression by 100 to get a percentage. So the correct choice is (B).

7. **(D)**

⑧

Difficulty Level

Set up a coordinate system with A at (0, 0). Then B is at (5, 0). Since C is southeast of B, then BCD is an isosceles right triangle whose hypotenuse is 10 miles. So $BD^2 + CD^2 = 10^2 = 100$ and $BD = CD$, so $BD^2 = 50$. Therefore, $BD = \sqrt{50} = \sqrt{25}\sqrt{2} = 5\sqrt{2}$. So the coordinates of C are $(5 + 5\sqrt{2}, -5\sqrt{2})$. Remember, the distance between two points whose coordinates are (x, y) and (a, b) is $\sqrt{(x-a)^2 + (y-b)^2}$. So the distance from A to C is the square root of $(5 + 5\sqrt{2})^2 + (-5\sqrt{2})^2$. You can work with these numbers, but it will be messy. It is much faster to use the fact that $\sqrt{2}$ is about 1.4. Remember, the question asks for only an approximate answer.

So $5\sqrt{2}$ is about 7; thus, the distance is the square root of $(5 + 7)^2 + (-7)^2$. This is equal to the square root of $144 + 49$ or 193. *Do not try to find the square root of this number if you don't know it.* Simply square each answer and see which is closest to 193. Since $14^2 = 196$, the correct choice is 14 miles or (D).

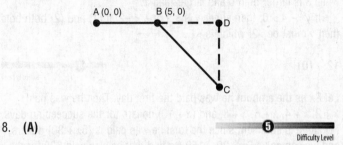

8. **(A)**

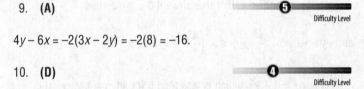

Difficulty Level

If 40 percent of the socks are blue, then we can see that there are $12(.4 \times 30)$ blue socks in the drawer. So the probability that both socks are blue is $\left(\dfrac{12}{30}\right)\left(\dfrac{11}{29}\right)$ and STATEMENT 1 is sufficient.

STATEMENT 2 is not sufficient since it does not tell us how many blue socks are in the drawer. You don't know that all the socks are either red or blue because there could be socks of other colors in the drawer.

9. **(A)**

Difficulty Level

$4y - 6x = -2(3x - 2y) = -2(8) = -16.$

10. **(D)**

Difficulty Level

Since the total distance is 200 kilometers, of which you fly x kilometers, you drive $(200 - x)$ kilometers. Therefore, the cost is $10x + (200 - x)12$, which is $10x - 12x + 2,400$ or $2,400 - 2x$ cents. The answer in dollars is obtained by dividing by 100, which is $(24 - .02x)$ dollars.

11. **(C)**

(2) alone is not sufficient since both $y = 3$ and $y = -3$ satisfy $y^2 - 4 > 0$.

(1) alone is not sufficient, since $\frac{1}{2}$ is larger than 0 but less than 1,

while 3 is larger than 0 and larger than 1.

   If $y^2 - 4 > 0$, then either y is > 2 or $y < -2$. If (1) and (2) both hold, then y must be >2, which is >1.

12. **(D)**

Let $\$x$ be the amount he was paid the first day. Then he was paid $x + 2$, $x + 4$, $x + 6$, $x + 8$, and $(x + 10)$ dollars for the succeeding days. (1) alone is sufficient since the total he was paid is $(6x + 30)$ dollars, and we can solve $6x + 30 = 150$ (to find that he was paid $20 for the first day). (2) alone is also sufficient. He was paid $(x + 10)$ dollars on the sixth day, so (2) means that $(1.5)x = x + 10$ (which is the same as $x = 20$).

13. **(D)**

I is not true for all positive y since $*1 = 4 - 1 = 3$, which is not negative. The question asks which statements are true for *all positive y*,

not just some positive y. II is true since if $0 < y < z$, then $\frac{4}{y} > \frac{4}{z}$

and $-y > -z$, so $\left(\frac{4}{y}\right) - y$ is $> \left(\frac{4}{z}\right) - z$. So $*y > *z$. Since $y(*y) =$

$y\left[\left(\frac{4}{y}\right) - y\right] = 4 - y^2$, which is less than 5 for any positive y, III is

always true. So the correct answer is (D).

14. **(B)**

Since 85 percent of $3,000 is $2,550, (2) alone is sufficient. (1) alone is not sufficient since if x were 5 percent, (1) would tell us that the price of the car is less than $2,600. But if x were 1 percent, (1) would imply that the price of the car is greater than $2,600.

15. **(E)**

Difficulty Level

Even assuming (1) and (2), you would still need to know what percentage of birds have avian flu in order to answer the question. Since that information is not available, both statements together are not sufficient.

16. **(B)**

Difficulty Level

If A_1 denotes the increased area and A the original area, then $A_1 = 1.69A$ since A_1 is A increased by 69 percent. Thus, $s_1^2 = A_1 = 1.69A = 1.69s^2$, where s_1 is the increased side and s the original side. Since the square root of 1.69 is 1.3, we have $s_1 = 1.3s$ so s is increased by .3 or 30 percent.

17. **(A)**

Difficulty Level

I can be inferred since the average number of hours worked is $\frac{3,100}{80} = 38.75$, which is less than 40. II cannot be inferred since there is no information given beyond the fact that 20 workers worked between 45 and 50 hours. Since only 35 workers worked 40 or more hours, III cannot be inferred.

18. **(B)**

Difficulty Level

To calculate the driving time, simply divide 160 miles by 60 miles per hour to obtain $2\frac{2}{3}$ hours, or 160 minutes. However, you need to decide whether or not the truck must stop for gasoline. At a speed of 60 miles per hour, the truck will use 30 percent more fuel, so it will need 1.3 gallons to travel 20 miles. Thus x (the amount of fuel needed to travel 160 miles) must satisfy the proportion $\frac{160}{20} = \frac{x}{1.3}$

or $x = 8(1.3) = 10.4$ gallons. So, if the truck is driven at 60 miles per hour, it will have to stop for gas since it has only 10 gallons. Therefore, the total time needed is $160 + 20 = 180$ minutes.

19. **(C)**

Difficulty Level

If company C owns 25 percent more than company A and A owns 40 percent of XYZ Corporation, then company C must own $1.25 \times .4 = .5$, or 50 percent of XYZ Corporation. Since B owns all that A and C do not own, then B must own $100\% - 40\% - 50\% = 10\%$.

If 10 percent of the shares is 15,000 shares, then there must be 150,000 shares in XYZ Corporation. Since company A owns 40 percent, it owns $150,000 \times 0.40 = 60,000$ shares. So (C) is the correct answer. Remember: Always answer the question asked. If you picked (D), you found only how many shares company C owns.

20. **(D)**

Difficulty Level

The area of the rectangle is $4 \times 6 = 24$ square feet. Since 1 square foot is 144 square inches, the area of the rectangle is 3,456 square inches. Each square has an area of $\left(\dfrac{1}{2}\right)^2$ or $\dfrac{1}{4}$ square inches. Therefore, the number of squares needed $= 3,456 \div \dfrac{1}{4} = 3,456 \times 4 = 13,824$.

21. **(D)**

Difficulty Level

Since there are a bottom and 4 sides, each a congruent square, the amount of cardboard needed will be $5e^2$, where e is the length of an edge of the box. So we need to find e.

(1) alone is sufficient. Since the area of the bottom is e^2, (1) means $e^2 = 4$ with $e = 2$ feet. (2) alone is also sufficient. Since the volume of the box is e^3, (2) means $e^3 = 8$ and $e = 2$ feet.

22. **(B)**

Difficulty Level

STATEMENT (1) is not sufficient. If x is 33, then (1) is true and x is divisible by 3, but if x is 23, then (1) is true but x is not divisible by 3.

STATEMENT (2) is sufficient. According to (2) there must be an integer k such that $x + 5 = 6k$, so x is $6k - 5$. But this means that x divided by 3 will be $2k - \left(\dfrac{5}{3}\right)$, so x is not divisible by 3.

So (B) is the correct choice.

23. **(E)**

Difficulty Level

If *ABCD* has the pairs of opposite sides equal and each angle is 90°, then it is a rectangle. But there are many quadrilaterals that have two opposite sides equal with one angle a right angle. For example, the figure below has $AB = DC$ and $x = 90$, but it is not a rectangle. Therefore, (1) and (2) together are insufficient.

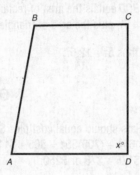

24. **(D)**

Difficulty Level

(2) alone is sufficient since if $a_3 = 1$, then $a_4 = (a_3)^2 = 1^2 = 1$; then $a_5 = (a_4)^2 = 1^2 = 1$. (1) alone is also sufficient. If $a_1 = -1$, then $a_2 = (a_1)^2 = 1$ and $a_3 = (a_2)^2 = 1$, but $a_3 = 1$ is given by (2), which we know is sufficient.

25. **(E)**

Difficulty Level

Those who gave \$12 were 25 percent ($100\% - 30\% - 45\% = 25\%$) of the group. Let *x*, *y*, and *z* stand for the number of people who contributed \$40, \$20, and \$12, respectively. Then, the total number of people (*n*) who contributed is $x + y + z = n$. The total amount (*T*) contributed is

$$\$40x + \$20y + \$12z = T$$

Since 30 percent contributed \$40, we know that $x = .3n$; in the same way, we know that $y = .45n$ and $z = .25n$. Therefore, the total contributed was

$$
\begin{aligned}
T &= \$40(.3n) &+ \$20(.45n) &+ \$12(.25n) \\
&= 12n &+ 9n &+ 3n \\
&= 24n
\end{aligned}
$$

The amount contributed by those who gave $40 was, therefore,

$$\$40\,(.3n) = 12n$$

So the percentage contributed by the $40 donors is $100(12n/24n)$ or 50 percent.

26. (A)

6
Difficulty Level

The area of trapezoid $ABCD$ equals the area of rectangle $ABED$, which is $t \times 5$ (since $BE = BC = 5$), plus the area of triangle BEC, which is $\frac{(5 \times 5)}{2}$. The answer is thus $5t + 12.5$.

27. (E)

3
Difficulty Level

The selling price of the jars should equal cost plus $75. The cost of making 300 jars = $(100)65¢ + (200)55¢ = \$65 + \$110 = \$175$. So the selling price should be $175 + 75$ or $250.

28. (E)

7
Difficulty Level

You need to find the total distance traveled in order to find the total time. Since the car traveled $V \times T$ miles when it averaged V miles per hour, then VT is 75 percent of the total distance. Therefore, the total distance traveled is $\frac{VT}{.75} = \frac{4VT}{3}$.

The distance that was traveled at S miles per hour is the total distance minus the distance at V miles per hour, which is

$$\left(\frac{4}{3}\right)VT - VT = \frac{VT}{3}$$

So the time spent traveling at S miles per hour was $(VT)/3 \div S = \frac{VT}{3S}$.

29. (E)

4
Difficulty Level

Let J, F, and C stand for the weekly salaries of John, Fred, and Chuck. (1) says $J = 2F$, and (2) says $F = .4(C + J)$. Since there is no information given about the value of C or F, we cannot deduce the value of J. Therefore, (1) and (2) together are insufficient.

30. **(B)**

Difficulty Level

STATEMENT (2) alone is sufficient. $2x + 4y = 2(x + 2y)$, so if $2x + 4y = 12$, then $2(x + 2y) = 12$ and $x + 2y = 6$.

STATEMENT (1) alone is insufficient. If you use only STATEMENT (1), then you can get $x + 2y = x + y + y = 4 + y$, but there is no information on the value of y.

31. **(C)**

Difficulty Level

Since the sum of the angles in a triangle is 180°, $x + y + z = 180$. Using STATEMENT (1) alone, we have $2y + y + z = 3y + z = 180$, which is insufficient to determine y or z.

Using STATEMENT (2) alone, we have $x + 1.5z + z = x + 2.5z = 180$, which is not sufficient to determine x or z.

However, if we use both STATEMENTS (1) and (2) we obtain $3y + z = 4.5z + z = 5.5z = 180$, so $z = \frac{2}{11}$ of 180. Now $y = \frac{3}{2}$ of z, so $y = \frac{3}{11}$ of 180, and $x = \frac{6}{11}$ of 180. Therefore, angle BAC is not a right angle and STATEMENTS (1) and (2) are sufficient.

32. **(A)**

Difficulty Level

The three-digit number abc is $(100 \times a) + (10 \times b) + c$. If abc is a multiple of 9, then there is an integer k such that $k9 = (100 \times a) + (10 \times b) + c$. Divide this equation by 9 and you have

$$k = \left[\left(\frac{100}{9}\right) \times a\right] + \left[\left(\frac{10}{9}\right) \times b\right] + \frac{c}{9}$$

$$= \left[11a + \left(\frac{a}{9}\right)\right] + \left[b + \left(\frac{b}{9}\right)\right] + \frac{c}{9}$$

$$= 11a + b + \left(\frac{a}{9}\right) + \left(\frac{b}{9}\right) + \left(\frac{c}{9}\right)$$

$$= 11a + b + \left[\left(\frac{a + b + c}{9}\right)\right]$$

So (1) alone is sufficient. (2) is not sufficient since choosing $a = 0 = b$ and $c = 9$ makes (2) valid and $a + b + c$ is 9, but choosing $a = 4 = b$ and $c = 2$ also makes (2) valid with $a + b + c$ equal to 10.

33. **(B)**

Difficulty Level

STATEMENT (2) alone is sufficient. 60 percent of the people have blue eyes and 50 percent of the people have blue eyes and blond hair, so 60% − 50% = 10% of the people have blue eyes but do not have blond hair.

STATEMENT (1) alone is not sufficient. Using STATEMENT (1) alone we can only find out how many people have blond hair and do not have blue eyes, in addition to what is given.

34. **(C)**

Difficulty Level

Let c be the number of chairs in a row and r be the number of rows. Since each row must have the same number of chairs, c times r must equal 36. We need to know how many ways we can write 36 as a product of two integers each greater than or equal to 3, since each way to write 36 corresponds to an acceptable arrangement of the room. (c must be greater than or equal to 3 since each row must contain at least 3 chairs. In the same way, r must be greater than or equal to 3 because there must be at least 3 rows.) Writing 36 as a product of primes, we obtain $36 = 2 \times 18 = 2 \times 2 \times 9 = 2 \times 2 \times 3 \times 3$. So 36 can be written as 1×36, 2×18, 3×12, 4×9, 6×6, 9×4, 12×3, 18×2, and 36×1. Of these possibilities, five (3×12, 4×9, 6×6, 9×4, and 12×3) satisfy the requirements. Therefore, there are five arrangements.

35. **(B)**

Difficulty Level

The volume of the cube is $9 \times 9 \times 9 = 729$ cubic millimeters. The sphere has volume $\frac{4}{3}\pi 6 \times 6 \times 6 = 288\pi$. Since π is greater than 3, 288π is greater than 729. The volume of the cylinder is $5 \times 5 \times 11\pi = 275\pi$. So the sphere has the largest volume.

You can save a lot of time in doing this problem if you do not change π to a decimal and then multiply the answers out.

36. **(A)**

Difficulty Level

The sum of the angles of the pentagon is 540°. [The sum of the angles of a polygon with n sides that is inscribed in a circle is $(n-2)180°$.]

STATEMENT (1) alone is sufficient. If the polygon is regular, all angles are equal, and so angle ABC is $\frac{1}{5}$ of 540° or 108°.

STATEMENT (2) alone is insufficient because the radius of the circle does not give any information about the angles of the pentagon.

37. **(C)**

Difficulty Level

The key to this problem is to factor $k^2 + k - 2$ into $(k+2)(k-1)$. The product of the two expressions is positive if and only if both expressions have the same sign. When (1) holds, then $k-1$ is negative, but $k+2$ can be positive or negative, so (1) alone is not sufficient. When (2) holds, then $k+2$ is positive, but $k-1$ can be positive or negative, so (2) alone is not sufficient. However, if both (1) and (2) are true, then k is between -1 and 1 and, so $k+2$ is positive and $k-1$ is negative, which means $(k+2)(k-1)$ is negative. This is sufficient to answer the question.

Verbal Section

1. **(B)**

Difficulty Level

The argument represents a fallacy in causality. Absence of cloud cover enables the moon to be seen. And, it is the absence of cloud cover— not a full moon—that causes the ground to cool and produce frost. Answer choice (A) may be a necessary but insufficient condition for frost to occur; that is, there may be an absence of frost even below 10 degrees Celsius. Farmers may be superstitious, but there is nothing in the statement that links superstition with the farmers' conviction (alternative C). Alternative (D) is inappropriate because, even if true, it could not change the farmers' convictions. Farmers do not have to be experts in meteorology (E) to hold a conviction.

2. **(B)**

Difficulty Level

The question concerns Professor Tembel's proposal to improve the validity of the method used to measure teacher quality. Alternative (B) supports the proposal. Students relate only partial experience with a teacher if the questionnaires are completed at midterm. Alternative (A) suggests that Professor Tembel's motive for questioning the present evaluation method stems from his low ratings. It is questionable whether handing out questionnaires at the end of the semester would improve his ratings. Alternatives (C), (D), and (E) are not related to the validity of the evaluation method.

3. **(B)**

Difficulty Level

This corrects the misuse of the subjunctive.

4. **(D)**

Difficulty Level

This corrects the error in the case of the pronoun. Choice E corrects the error in case but introduces an error in tense.

5. **(D)**

Difficulty Level

This is clearly a passage dealing with the economy and economic pol-icy. Note that (E) is too vague; an *economic policy* textbook might have been a correct answer.

6. **(E)**

Difficulty Level

All of the others are given in paragraph 1.

7. **(C)**

Difficulty Level

See paragraph 3. The task is to obtain high economic growth without stimulating high inflation.

8. **(B)**

Difficulty Level

See paragraph 2: ". . . there was actually a substantial deterioration in our trade account to a sizable deficit, almost two thirds of which was with Japan."

9. **(C)**

Difficulty Level

The improper use of the pronouns one and you is corrected in Choice C.

10. **(E)**
Difficulty Level

The omission of the past participle been is corrected in Choice E.

11. **(D)**
Difficulty Level

All of the facts except (D) would be consonant with the President's actions. Fact (D) would be against passage of such a bill.

12. **(E)**
Difficulty Level

The argument is in the form of a conditional syllogism: (1) *If* we must have drug rehabilitation centers, *then* society ought to pay for them. (2) We must have drug rehabilitation centers. (3) Society ought to pay for them. Alternative (E) falsifies the minor premise 2. Whether or not neighborhood groups oppose the centers (B) or drug addicts will go to them to receive treatment (D) is not relevant to the argument concerning who will pay for them. The level of government funding (A) or the amount of expense (C) are not mentioned in the passage and are not relevant to the argument. However, a government statement that local rehabilitation centers are ineffective would seriously weaken the premise upon which the argument rests.

13. **(B)**

Difficulty Level ⑤

See paragraph 1: "Under a perfectly sunny sky and from an apparently calm sea . . ." None of the other answer choices is particularly surprising.

14. **(C)**

Difficulty Level ④

See the first sentence of the passage: ". . . distant lands or continents."

15. **(D)**

Difficulty Level ③

See paragraph 2: "How are these waves formed? When a submarine earthquake occurs . . ."

16. **(A)**

Difficulty Level ⑥

While (B) and (E) suggest desirable actions, they are not mentioned in the passage. (C) and (D) provide far less information than alternative (A).

17. **(A)**

Difficulty Level ⑥

No error.

18. **(D)**

Difficulty Level ⑦

Misuse of word. The pronoun is *its*.

19. **(B)**

Difficulty Level ⑤

This corrects the unnecessary switch in the pronouns, *anyone—you*.

20. **(D)**

Difficulty Level ④

This corrects the error in tense and in the use of adjective or adverbial clauses.

21. **(A)**

Difficulty Level

No error.

22. **(B)**

Difficulty Level

The "crisis" which is alluded to in the statement refers to a need for environmental clean-up and basic human services (the latter mentioned in alternative (E)). In order to provide these services more workers will be needed (C), many of whom will have to be retrained. This retraining will have to be financed by subsidies (A), which may be provided by the private sector (D). Alternative (B) is inconsistent with the statement which calls for more environmental controls (clean-up), not less.

23. **(E)**

Difficulty Level

Total per-capita income includes salaries and wages earned by women. In order to determine if women wage-earners earned more than the overall average, the salaries of all women—not just women heading families with no husband present—would have to be calculated separately. Alternative (E) states that women family heads are not representative of all women wage earners. Thus, the conclusion in the statement is a fallacy of relevance or representativeness. All other alternatives would buttress the conclusion.

24. **(C)**

Difficulty Level

The correct answer is given in paragraph 2. The policeman must be neutral and present the facts, while the "artist usually begins with a preconceived message or attitude . . . ," i.e., prejudiced. While artists are "emotional," no mention is made that policemen are stoic (D).

25. **(A)**

Difficulty Level

The writer explains that the policemen's reactions were "surprisingly unprejudiced." The rest of paragraph 3 explains that policemen reacted to story events and characters according to alternative (A).

26. **(A)**

6 Difficulty Level

The only characters that policemen objected to were unrealistic. See paragraph 3.

27. **(C)**

6 Difficulty Level

Alternatives I and II may be found in the first paragraph.

28. **(D)**

5 Difficulty Level

Land values were higher in Europe, attracting U.S. capital (A); higher duties on U.S. exports to Europe (B) brought a substitution of foreign production for U.S. exports; lower labor costs in Europe (C) meant it was cheaper to produce there. Higher liquidity (E) in the U.S. provided the capital for foreign investment. Only (D) is irrelevant as an explanation of direct investment.

29. **(A)**

9 Difficulty Level

A number of points are made in the paragraph, and a number of conclusions can be drawn. One is (B), the simple law of economics—that demand varies with price. Also, since it is stated that there is now an increasing tendency to have the January sales in December, it must be becoming less popular to start the sales in January itself. Therefore, the conclusions in (C) and (D) can be drawn, and so choices (C) and (D) are not appropriate. Further, the hypothesis in (C) and also in (E) can be inferred from what is stated in the paragraph about the stores' policies on end-of-year sales. Answer choice (A) introduces a new idea that may be correct and valid, but which cannot be inferred or concluded from what is stated in the paragraph; (A), therefore is the correct answer.

30. **(E)**

8 Difficulty Level

The reason is that is preferable to *The reason is because.*

31. **(D)**

5 Difficulty Level

This corrects the double negative (*hadn't hardly*) and the misuse of *those* with *kind.*

32. **(B)**
Difficulty Level

This corrects the dangling participle and the misuse of *stole* for *stolen*.

33. **(E)**
Difficulty Level

This question involves two aspects of correct English. *Neither* should be followed by *nor*, *either* by *or*. Choices A and D are, therefore, incorrect. The words *neither . . . nor* and *either . . . or* should be placed before the two items being discussed—*to be critical* and *to criticize*. Choice E meets both requirements.

34. **(B)**
Difficulty Level

This question tests agreement. Agreement between subject and verb and pronoun and antecedent are both involved. *Community* (singular) needs a singular verb, *influences*. Also, the pronoun which refers to *community* should be singular (*its*). Choice B is best.

35. **(A)**
Difficulty Level

Two of the three countries actually experienced shifts in their share of world external-debt from 1990 to 1999, hardly an example of stability. Answer choice (B) may be true for some countries, but it does not weaken the statement. Answer choices (C) and (D) skirt the issues: rates of economic growth and absolute debt are not related to external debt in the statement. Answer choice (E) may be so, but the example in the statement deals with external, not internal, debt.

36. **(B)**
Difficulty Level

The argument claims that fewer cars on the road will lead to fewer accidents. In order to hold down the existing number of cars, it is suggested that custom taxes not be reduced so as not to lower the price to the consumer. Statement I does not weaken the claim because it does not refute the fact of a high incidence of traffic accidents. Statement III strengthens the claim. A higher volume of cars on an inadequate road network should lead to more accidents. Statement II weakens the argument because it provides evidence that even if car prices were reduced it would not lead to increased purchases, which, of course, is the argument in the passage.

37. **(E)**
Difficulty Level

Statements (A) and (B) do not address themselves to the premise or conclusion. The conclusion in the statement is that smoking is benefi-cial. Why? Because it leads to longevity through greater relaxation as a result of smoking. Statement (C) is true, but it does not attack the premise. Statement (D) does attack the premise of the beneficiality of smoking, but it does not give evidence of harm. Statement (E) throws doubt on the major premise, and thus on the conclusion.

38. **(B)**
Difficulty Level

The claim in the statement is that the CPI will go up. The reasoning behind the claim is based on the premise that the cost of fruit and vegetables has risen sharply (A). Since these commodities are major items in the CPI (C) and because food cost changes are reflected quickly in the index (D), the index will go up. A premise that could weaken the claim might be (E) if other items included in the index and weighted at least as much decreased in price, thus offsetting the cost increases for fruits and vegetables. However, alternative (E) gives evidence to the contrary. Alternative (B) may not be inferred. If con-sumers reduced consumption of fruits and vegetables, the prices of these items would be expected to drop. In any case, the rate of con-sumption cannot be inferred.

39. **(B)**
Difficulty Level

If the behavior at the rally is indicative of how people will vote *and* the rally attendance was representative of the voters, then the conclusion is valid. The argument is thus: (1) The rally is representative of all vot-ers. (2) Most at the rally are for me. (3) Most rally attendees will vote for me. Alternative (A) might also support the conclusion since even with the appearance of the opponent, Smith says "Nearly everyone at the rally is behind me," but this support depends on whether or not the people at the rally are voters in the election, so this is not the best answer. Smith's previous election results (C) or support from the mayor (D) are not relevant to the conclusion. Alternative (E) is also irrelevant; support at a rally does not imply only emotional support.

40. **(B)**

6
Difficulty Level

As presented, the sentence contains a dangling participle, *depending*. Choice B corrects this error. The other choices change the emphasis presented by the author.

41. **(C)**

3
Difficulty Level

In this experiment, the dog was conditioned to associate the ringing of a bell with food. Therefore, when the dog heard the bell, it expected to be fed, even though it could not smell food. Alternative (A) cannot be inferred. Alternative (B) and (D) are incorrect, and there is no proof for (E).

EVALUATING YOUR SCORE

Tabulate your score for each section of the Sample Test and record the results in the Self-Scoring Table below. (See page 7.) Then find your rating for each score on the Self-Scoring Scale.

SELF-SCORING TABLE		
Section	Score	Rating
Quantitative		
Verbal		

SELF-SCORING SCALE—RATING				
Section	Poor	Fair	Good	Excellent
Quantitative	0–15	15–25	26–30	31–37
Verbal	0–15	15–25	26–30	31–41

Answer Sheet—Sample Test 2

Quantitative Section

1 Ⓐ Ⓑ Ⓒ Ⓓ Ⓔ   15 Ⓐ Ⓑ Ⓒ Ⓓ Ⓔ   29 Ⓐ Ⓑ Ⓒ Ⓓ Ⓔ
2 Ⓐ Ⓑ Ⓒ Ⓓ Ⓔ   16 Ⓐ Ⓑ Ⓒ Ⓓ Ⓔ   30 Ⓐ Ⓑ Ⓒ Ⓓ Ⓔ
3 Ⓐ Ⓑ Ⓒ Ⓓ Ⓔ   17 Ⓐ Ⓑ Ⓒ Ⓓ Ⓔ   31 Ⓐ Ⓑ Ⓒ Ⓓ Ⓔ
4 Ⓐ Ⓑ Ⓒ Ⓓ Ⓔ   18 Ⓐ Ⓑ Ⓒ Ⓓ Ⓔ   32 Ⓐ Ⓑ Ⓒ Ⓓ Ⓔ
5 Ⓐ Ⓑ Ⓒ Ⓓ Ⓔ   19 Ⓐ Ⓑ Ⓒ Ⓓ Ⓔ   33 Ⓐ Ⓑ Ⓒ Ⓓ Ⓔ
6 Ⓐ Ⓑ Ⓒ Ⓓ Ⓔ   20 Ⓐ Ⓑ Ⓒ Ⓓ Ⓔ   34 Ⓐ Ⓑ Ⓒ Ⓓ Ⓔ
7 Ⓐ Ⓑ Ⓒ Ⓓ Ⓔ   21 Ⓐ Ⓑ Ⓒ Ⓓ Ⓔ   35 Ⓐ Ⓑ Ⓒ Ⓓ Ⓔ
8 Ⓐ Ⓑ Ⓒ Ⓓ Ⓔ   22 Ⓐ Ⓑ Ⓒ Ⓓ Ⓔ   36 Ⓐ Ⓑ Ⓒ Ⓓ Ⓔ
9 Ⓐ Ⓑ Ⓒ Ⓓ Ⓔ   23 Ⓐ Ⓑ Ⓒ Ⓓ Ⓔ   37 Ⓐ Ⓑ Ⓒ Ⓓ Ⓔ
10 Ⓐ Ⓑ Ⓒ Ⓓ Ⓔ   24 Ⓐ Ⓑ Ⓒ Ⓓ Ⓔ
11 Ⓐ Ⓑ Ⓒ Ⓓ Ⓔ   25 Ⓐ Ⓑ Ⓒ Ⓓ Ⓔ
12 Ⓐ Ⓑ Ⓒ Ⓓ Ⓔ   26 Ⓐ Ⓑ Ⓒ Ⓓ Ⓔ
13 Ⓐ Ⓑ Ⓒ Ⓓ Ⓔ   27 Ⓐ Ⓑ Ⓒ Ⓓ Ⓔ
14 Ⓐ Ⓑ Ⓒ Ⓓ Ⓔ   28 Ⓐ Ⓑ Ⓒ Ⓓ Ⓔ

Verbal Section

1 Ⓐ Ⓑ Ⓒ Ⓓ Ⓔ   15 Ⓐ Ⓑ Ⓒ Ⓓ Ⓔ   29 Ⓐ Ⓑ Ⓒ Ⓓ Ⓔ
2 Ⓐ Ⓑ Ⓒ Ⓓ Ⓔ   16 Ⓐ Ⓑ Ⓒ Ⓓ Ⓔ   30 Ⓐ Ⓑ Ⓒ Ⓓ Ⓔ
3 Ⓐ Ⓑ Ⓒ Ⓓ Ⓔ   17 Ⓐ Ⓑ Ⓒ Ⓓ Ⓔ   31 Ⓐ Ⓑ Ⓒ Ⓓ Ⓔ
4 Ⓐ Ⓑ Ⓒ Ⓓ Ⓔ   18 Ⓐ Ⓑ Ⓒ Ⓓ Ⓔ   32 Ⓐ Ⓑ Ⓒ Ⓓ Ⓔ
5 Ⓐ Ⓑ Ⓒ Ⓓ Ⓔ   19 Ⓐ Ⓑ Ⓒ Ⓓ Ⓔ   33 Ⓐ Ⓑ Ⓒ Ⓓ Ⓔ
6 Ⓐ Ⓑ Ⓒ Ⓓ Ⓔ   20 Ⓐ Ⓑ Ⓒ Ⓓ Ⓔ   34 Ⓐ Ⓑ Ⓒ Ⓓ Ⓔ
7 Ⓐ Ⓑ Ⓒ Ⓓ Ⓔ   21 Ⓐ Ⓑ Ⓒ Ⓓ Ⓔ   35 Ⓐ Ⓑ Ⓒ Ⓓ Ⓔ
8 Ⓐ Ⓑ Ⓒ Ⓓ Ⓔ   22 Ⓐ Ⓑ Ⓒ Ⓓ Ⓔ   36 Ⓐ Ⓑ Ⓒ Ⓓ Ⓔ
9 Ⓐ Ⓑ Ⓒ Ⓓ Ⓔ   23 Ⓐ Ⓑ Ⓒ Ⓓ Ⓔ   37 Ⓐ Ⓑ Ⓒ Ⓓ Ⓔ
10 Ⓐ Ⓑ Ⓒ Ⓓ Ⓔ   24 Ⓐ Ⓑ Ⓒ Ⓓ Ⓔ   38 Ⓐ Ⓑ Ⓒ Ⓓ Ⓔ
11 Ⓐ Ⓑ Ⓒ Ⓓ Ⓔ   25 Ⓐ Ⓑ Ⓒ Ⓓ Ⓔ   39 Ⓐ Ⓑ Ⓒ Ⓓ Ⓔ
12 Ⓐ Ⓑ Ⓒ Ⓓ Ⓔ   26 Ⓐ Ⓑ Ⓒ Ⓓ Ⓔ   40 Ⓐ Ⓑ Ⓒ Ⓓ Ⓔ
13 Ⓐ Ⓑ Ⓒ Ⓓ Ⓔ   27 Ⓐ Ⓑ Ⓒ Ⓓ Ⓔ   41 Ⓐ Ⓑ Ⓒ Ⓓ Ⓔ
14 Ⓐ Ⓑ Ⓒ Ⓓ Ⓔ   28 Ⓐ Ⓑ Ⓒ Ⓓ Ⓔ

SAMPLE TEST 2

WRITING ASSESSMENT

Part I   TIME: 30 MINUTES

> **Directions:** Write a clear, logical, and well-organized response to the following issue or argument. Your response should be in the form of a short essay, following the conventions of standard written English. Your answer should fit on three pages of lined 8½" × 11" paper or equivalent on your PC. Write legibly. Essays that are illegible or that are written on a topic other than the one outlined in the question will not be scored.

Forced obsolescence is a strategy that manufacturers use to limit the useful life of some consumer products in order to increase sales. Some commentators complain that this practice results in a waste of resources. What they do not understand is that by shortening the life cycle of products, manufacturers are able to both improve them and lower the cost to the consumer.

Which do you find more convincing: that forced obsolescence wastes resources or that it benefits consumers? State your position using relevant reasons from your own experience, observation, or reading.

IF THERE IS STILL TIME REMAINING, YOU MAY REVIEW YOUR ANSWER. AFTER YOU HAVE CONFIRMED YOUR ANSWER, YOU CANNOT RETURN TO THIS QUESTION.

Part II   TIME: 30 MINUTES

Directions: Write a clear, logical, and well-organized response to the following issue or argument. Your response should be in the form of a short essay, following the conventions of standard written English. Your answer should fit on three pages of lined 8½" × 11" paper or equivalent on your PC. Write legibly. Essays that are illegible or that are written on a topic other than the one outlined in the question will not be scored.

Women are more fashion-conscious than men. Women's clothing styles change ever year, forcing them update their wardrobes so as not to appear behind the times.

Discuss how logically persuasive you find the above argument. In presenting your point of view, analyze the sort of reasoning used and supporting evidence. In addition, state what further evidence, if any, would make the argument more sound and convincing or would make you better able to evaluate its conclusion.

IF THERE IS STILL TIME REMAINING, YOU MAY REVIEW YOUR ANSWER. AFTER YOU HAVE CONFIRMED YOUR ANSWER, YOU CANNOT RETURN TO THIS QUESTION.

QUANTITATIVE SECTION

TIME: 75 MINUTES

37 QUESTIONS

This section consists of two types of questions: Problem Solving and Data Sufficiency.

Problem Solving
Directions: Solve each of the following problems; then indicate the correct answer.

NOTE: A figure that appears with a problem is drawn as accurately as possible so as to provide information that may help in answering the question.
Numbers in this test are real numbers.

Data Sufficiency
Directions: Each of the following problems has a question and two state-ments which are labeled (1) and (2). Use the data given in (1) and (2) together with other available information (such as the number of hours in a day, the definition of *clockwise*, mathematical facts, etc.) to decide whether the statements are *sufficient* to answer the question. Then fill in space

(A) If you can get the answer from **(1) ALONE** but not from (2) alone
(B) If you can get the answer from **(2) ALONE** but not from (1) alone
(C) If you can get the answer from **BOTH (1) and (2) TOGETHER** but not from (1) alone or (2) alone
(D) If **EITHER** statement **(1) ALONE OR** statement **(2) ALONE** suffices
(E) If you **CANNOT** get the answer from statements (1) and (2) **TOGETHER** but need even more data

All numbers used in this section are real numbers.

A figure given for a problem is intended to provide information consis-tent with that in the question, but not necessarily with the additional information contained in the statements.
All figures lie in the plane unless you are told otherwise.
Figures are drawn as accurately as possible; straight lines may not appear straight on the screen.

1. Water has been poured into an empty rectangular tank at the rate of 5 cubic feet per minute for 6 minutes. The length of the tank is 4 feet and the width is $\frac{1}{2}$ of the length.

   How deep is the water in the tank?

   (A) 7.5 inches
   (B) 3 feet 7.5 inches
   (C) 3 feet 9 inches
   (D) 7 feet 6 inches
   (E) 30 feet

2. If x, y, z are chosen from the three numbers -3, $\frac{1}{2}$, and 2, what is the largest possible value of the expression $\left(\frac{x}{y}\right)z^2$?

   (A) $-\frac{3}{8}$

   (B) 16
   (C) 24
   (D) 36
   (E) 54

3. A survey of n people found that 60 percent preferred brand A. An additional x people were surveyed who all preferred brand A. Seventy percent of all the people surveyed preferred brand A. Find x in terms of n.

   (A) $\frac{n}{6}$

   (B) $\frac{n}{3}$

   (C) $\frac{n}{2}$

   (D) n
   (E) $3n$

(A) If you can get the answer from **(1) ALONE** but not from (2) alone
(B) If you can get the answer from **(2) ALONE** but not from (1) alone
(C) If you can get the answer from **BOTH (1) and (2) TOGETHER** but not from (1) alone or (2) alone
(D) If **EITHER** statement **(1) ALONE OR** statement **(2) ALONE** suffices
(E) If you **CANNOT** get the answer from statements (1) and (2) **TOGETHER** but need even more data

4. Is x greater than y?

   (1) $3x = 2k$
   (2) $k = y^2$

5. Is *ABCD* a parallelogram?

   (1) $AB = CD$
   (2) *AB* is parallel to *CD*

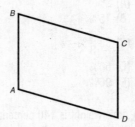

6. The hexagon *ABCDEF* is regular. That means all its sides are the same length and all its interior angles are the same size. Each side of the hexagon is 2 feet. What is the area of the rectangle *BCEF*?

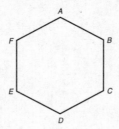

   (A) 4 square feet
   (B) $4\sqrt{3}$ square feet
   (C) 8 square feet
   (D) $4 + 4\sqrt{3}$ square feet
   (E) 12 square feet

(A) If you can get the answer from **(1) ALONE** but not from (2) alone

(B) If you can get the answer from **(2) ALONE** but not from (1) alone

(C) If you can get the answer from **BOTH (1) and (2) TOGETHER** but not from (1) alone or (2) alone

(D) If **EITHER** statement **(1) ALONE OR** statement **(2) ALONE** suffices

(E) If you **CANNOT** get the answer from statements (1) and (2) **TOGETHER** but need even more data

7. In Motor City 90 percent of the population own a car, 15 percent own a motorcycle, and everybody owns one or the other or both. What is the percentage of motorcycle owners who own cars?

   (A) 5%

   (B) 15%

   (C) $33\frac{1}{3}$%

   (D) 50%

   (E) 90%

8. Jim's weight is 140 percent of Marcia's weight. Bob's weight is 90 percent of Lee's weight. Lee weighs twice as much as Marcia. What percentage of Jim's weight is Bob's weight?

   (A) $64\frac{2}{7}$

   (B) $77\frac{7}{9}$

   (C) 90

   (D) $128\frac{4}{7}$

   (E) $155\frac{5}{9}$

9. What is the two-digit number whose first digit is a and whose second digit is b? The number is greater than 9.

   (1) $2a + 3b = 11a + 2b$

   (2) The two-digit number is a multiple of 19.

(A) If you can get the answer from **(1) ALONE** but not from (2) alone

(B) If you can get the answer from **(2) ALONE** but not from (1) alone

(C) If you can get the answer from **BOTH (1) and (2) TOGETHER** but not from (1) alone or (2) alone

(D) If **EITHER** statement **(1) ALONE OR** statement **(2) ALONE** suffices

(E) If you **CANNOT** get the answer from statements (1) and (2) **TOGETHER** but need even more data

10. A chair originally cost $50.00. The chair was offered for sale at 108 percent of its cost. After a week, the price was discounted 10 percent and the chair was sold. The chair was sold for

(A) $45.00

(B) $48.60

(C) $49.00

(D) $49.50

(E) $54.00

11. k is a positive integer. Is k a prime number?

(1) No integer between 2 and $\sqrt{k}$ inclusive, divides k evenly.

(2) No integer between 2 and $\dfrac{k}{2}$ inclusive, divides k evenly, and k is greater than 5.

12. Towns A and C are connected by a straight highway that is 60 miles long. The straight-line distance between town A and town B is 50 miles, and the straight-line distance from town B to town C is 50 miles. How many miles is it from town B to the point on the highway connecting towns A and C that is closest to town B?

(A) 30

(B) 40

(C) $30\sqrt{2}$

(D) 50

(E) 60

(A) If you can get the answer from **(1) ALONE** but not from (2) alone

(B) If you can get the answer from **(2) ALONE** but not from (1) alone

(C) If you can get the answer from **BOTH (1) and (2) TOGETHER** but not from (1) alone or (2) alone

(D) If **EITHER** statement **(1) ALONE OR** statement **(2) ALONE** suffices

(E) If you **CANNOT** get the answer from statements (1) and (2) **TOGETHER** but need even more data

13. A worker is paid x dollars for the first 8 hours he works each day. He is paid y dollars per hour for each hour he works in excess of 8 hours. During one week he works 8 hours on Monday, 11 hours on Tuesday, 9 hours on Wednesday, 10 hours on Thursday, and 9 hours on Friday. What is his average daily wage in dollars for the 5-day week?

    (A) $x + 1.4y$

    (B) $2x + y$

    (C) $\dfrac{(5x + 8y)}{5}$

    (D) $8x + 1.4y$

    (E) $5x + 7y$

14. A club has 8 male and 8 female members. The club is choosing a committee of 6 members. The committee must have 3 male and 3 female members. How many different committees can be chosen?

    (A) 112,896

    (B) 3,136

    (C) 720

    (D) 112

    (E) 9

15. The towns A, B, and C lie on a straight line. C is between A and B. The distance from A to B is 100 miles. How far is it from A to C?

    (1) The distance from A to B is 25 percent more than the distance from C to B.

    (2) The distance from A to C is $\dfrac{1}{4}$ of the distance from C to B.

(A) If you can get the answer from **(1) ALONE** but not from (2) alone

(B) If you can get the answer from **(2) ALONE** but not from (1) alone

(C) If you can get the answer from **BOTH (1) and (2) TOGETHER** but not from (1) alone or (2) alone

(D) If **EITHER** statement **(1) ALONE OR** statement **(2) ALONE** suffices

(E) If you **CANNOT** get the answer from statements (1) and (2) **TOGETHER** but need even more data

16. A club has 10 male and 5 female members. Each member of the club writes their name on a ticket, and the tickets are deposited in a box. The club chooses 2 members to go to a national meeting by drawing 2 tickets from the box. What is the probability that both members picked for the trip are female?

(A) $\dfrac{2}{21}$

(B) $\dfrac{1}{10}$

(C) $\dfrac{2}{7}$

(D) $\dfrac{5}{15}$

(E) $\dfrac{2}{5}$

17. The distribution of scores on a math test had a mean of 82 percent with a standard deviation of 5 percent. The score that is exactly 2 standard deviations above the mean is

(A) 72%

(B) 82%

(C) 92%

(D) 95%

(E) cannot be determined

18. What is the value of $x - y$?

(1) $x + 2y = 6$

(2) $x = y$

(A) If you can get the answer from **(1) ALONE** but not from (2) alone
(B) If you can get the answer from **(2) ALONE** but not from (1) alone
(C) If you can get the answer from **BOTH (1) and (2) TOGETHER** but not from (1) alone or (2) alone
(D) If **EITHER** statement **(1) ALONE OR** statement **(2) ALONE** suffices
(E) If you **CANNOT** get the answer from statements (1) and (2) **TOGETHER** but need even more data

19. The number of eligible voters is 100,000. How many eligible voters voted?

    (1) 63 percent of the eligible men voted.
    (2) 67 percent of the eligible women voted.

20. A motorcycle costs $2,500 when it is brand new. At the end of each year it is worth 80 percent of what it was worth at the beginning of the year. What is the motorcycle worth when it is 3 years old?

    (A) $1,000
    (B) $1,200
    (C) $1,280
    (D) $1,340
    (E) $1,430

21. Which of the following inequalities is the solution to the inequality $7x - 5 < 12x + 18$?

    (A) $x < -\dfrac{13}{5}$

    (B) $x > -\dfrac{23}{5}$

    (C) $x < -\dfrac{23}{5}$

    (D) $x > \dfrac{23}{5}$

    (E) $x < \dfrac{23}{5}$

(A) If you can get the answer from **(1) ALONE** but not from (2) alone
(B) If you can get the answer from **(2) ALONE** but not from (1) alone
(C) If you can get the answer from **BOTH (1) and (2) TOGETHER** but not from (1) alone or (2) alone
(D) If **EITHER** statement **(1) ALONE OR** statement **(2) ALONE** suffices
(E) If you **CANNOT** get the answer from statements (1) and (2) **TOGETHER** but need even more data

22. The hexagon *ABCDEF* is inscribed in the circle with center *O*. What is the length of *AB*?

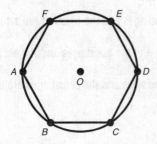

   (1) The radius of the circle is 4 inches.
   (2) The hexagon is a regular hexagon. That means all its sides are the same length and all its interior angles are the same size.

23. What was the percentage of defective items produced at a factory?

   (1) The total number of defective items produced was 1,234.
   (2) The ratio of defective items to nondefective items was 32 to 5,678.

(A) If you can get the answer from **(1) ALONE** but not from (2) alone

(B) If you can get the answer from **(2) ALONE** but not from (1) alone

(C) If you can get the answer from **BOTH (1) and (2) TOGETHER** but not from (1) alone or (2) alone

(D) If **EITHER** statement **(1) ALONE OR** statement **(2) ALONE** suffices

(E) If you **CANNOT** get the answer from statements (1) and (2) **TOGETHER** but need even more data

24. On a list of peoples ages the tabulator made an error that resulted in 20 years being added to each person's age. Which of the following statements is true.

   I. The mean of the listed ages and the mean of the actual ages are the same.

   II. The standard deviation of the listed ages and the actual ages are the same.

   III. The range of the listed ages and the actual ages are the same.

   (A) only II
   (B) I and II
   (C) I and III
   (D) II and III
   (E) I, II, and III

25. Is ABC a right triangle? $AB = 5$; $AC = 4$.

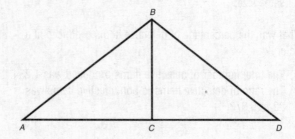

   (1) $BC = 3$
   (2) $AC = CD$

(A) If you can get the answer from **(1) ALONE** but not from (2) alone

(B) If you can get the answer from **(2) ALONE** but not from (1) alone

(C) If you can get the answer from **BOTH (1) and (2) TOGETHER** but not from (1) alone or (2) alone

(D) If **EITHER** statement **(1) ALONE OR** statement **(2) ALONE** suffices

(E) If you **CANNOT** get the answer from statements (1) and (2) **TOGETHER** but need even more data

26. Did the price of energy rise last year?

(1) If the price of energy rose last year, then the price of food would rise this year.

(2) The price of food rose this year.

27. Mary, John, and Karen ate lunch together. Karen's meal cost 50 percent more than John's meal and Mary's meal cost $\frac{5}{6}$ as much as Karen's meal. If Mary paid $2 more than John, how much was the total that the three of them paid?

(A) $28.33

(B) $30.00

(C) $35.00

(D) $37.50

(E) $40.00

28. A group of 49 consumers were offered a chance to subscribe to three magazines: *A*, *B*, and *C*. Thirty-eight of the consumers subscribed to at least one of the magazines. How many of the 49 consumers subscribed to exactly two of the magazines?

(1) Twelve of the 49 consumers subscribed to all three of the magazines.

(2) Twenty of the 49 consumers subscribed to magazine *A*.

29. Is *k* an odd integer?

(1) *k* is divisible by 3.

(2) The square root of *k* is an integer divisible by 3.

(A) If you can get the answer from **(1) ALONE** but not from (2) alone

(B) If you can get the answer from **(2) ALONE** but not from (1) alone

(C) If you can get the answer from **BOTH (1) and (2) TOGETHER** but not from (1) alone or (2) alone

(D) If **EITHER** statement **(1) ALONE OR** statement **(2) ALONE** suffices

(E) If you **CANNOT** get the answer from statements (1) and (2) **TOGETHER** but need even more data

30. If the angles of a triangle are in the ratio 1 : 2 : 2, the triangle

   (A) is isosceles
   (B) is obtuse
   (C) is a right triangle
   (D) is equilateral
   (E) has one angle greater than 80°

31. How much was a certain Rembrandt painting worth in January 1991?

   (1) In January 1997 the painting was worth $2 million.
   (2) Over the ten years 1988–1997 the painting increased in value by 10 percent each year.

32. A sequence of numbers a_1, a_2, a_3, . . . is given by the rule $a_n^2 = a_{n+1}$. Does 3 appear in the sequence?

   (1) $a_1 = 2$
   (2) $a_3 = 16$

33. A wall with no windows is 11 feet high and 20 feet long. A large roll of wallpaper costs $25 and will cover 60 square feet of wall. A small roll of wallpaper costs $6 and will cover 10 square feet of wall. What is the least cost for enough wallpaper to cover the wall?

   (A) $75
   (B) $99
   (C) $100
   (D) $120
   (E) $132

(A) If you can get the answer from **(1) ALONE** but not from (2) alone
(B) If you can get the answer from **(2) ALONE** but not from (1) alone
(C) If you can get the answer from **BOTH (1) and (2) TOGETHER** but
not from (1) alone or (2) alone
(D) If **EITHER** statement **(1) ALONE OR** statement **(2) ALONE** suffices
(E) If you **CANNOT** get the answer from statements (1) and (2)
TOGETHER but need even more data

34. A jar is filled with 60 marbles. All the marbles in the jar are either
red or green. What is the smallest number of marbles that must
be drawn from the jar in order to be certain that a red marble
is drawn?

(1) The ratio of red marbles to green marbles is 2 : 1.
(2) There are 20 green marbles in the jar.

35. Is $\frac{1}{x}$ greater than $\frac{1}{y}$?

(1) x is greater than 1.
(2) x is less than y.

36. Plane X flies at r miles per hour from A to B. Plane Y flies at S
miles per hour from B to A. Both planes take off at the same time.
Which plane flies at a faster rate? Town C is between A and B.

(1) C is closer to A than it is to B.
(2) Plane X flies over C before plane Y.

37. Is $\frac{x}{12} > \frac{y}{40}$?

(1) $10x > 3y$
(2) $12x < 4y$

*IF THERE IS STILL TIME REMAINING, YOU MAY
REVIEW YOUR ANSWER. AFTER YOU HAVE CONFIRMED
YOUR ANSWER, YOU CANNOT RETURN TO THIS QUESTION.*

VERBAL SECTION

TIME: 75 MINUTES
41 QUESTIONS

Reading Comprehension
Directions: This section contains three reading passages. You are to read each one carefully. When answering the questions, you *will* be allowed to refer back to the passages. The questions are based on what is *stated* or *implied* in each passage.

Critical Reasoning
Directions: For each question in this section, choose the best answer among the listed alternatives.

Sentence Correction
Directions: This part of the section consists of a number of sentences in each of which some part or the whole is underlined. Each sentence is followed by five alternative versions of the underlined portion. Select the alternative you consider both most correct and most effective according to the requirements of standard written English. Answer (A) is the same as the original version; if you think the original version is best, select answer (A).

In considering the answer choices, be attentive to matters of grammar, diction, and syntax, as well as clarity, precision, and fluency. Do not select an answer that alters the meaning of the original sentence.

Questions 1–4 are based on the following passage.

The main burden of assuring that the resources of the federal government are well managed falls on relatively few of the five million men and women whom it employs. Under the department and agency heads there are 8,600 political, career, military, and foreign
(5) service executives—the top managers and professionals—who exert major influence on the manner in which the rest are directed and utilized. Below their level there are other thousands with assignments of some managerial significance, but we believe that the line of demarcation selected is the best available for our pur-
(10) poses in this attainment.

There is no complete inventory of positions or people in federal service at this level. The lack may be explained by separate agency statutes and personnel systems, diffusion among so many special services, and absence of any central point (short of the President
(15) himself) with jurisdiction over all upper-level personnel of the government.

Top Presidential appointees, about 500 of them, bear the brunt of translating the philosophy and aims of the current administration into practical programs. This group includes the secretaries and
(20) assistant secretaries of cabinet departments, agency heads and their deputies, heads and members of boards and commissions with fixed terms, and chiefs and directors of major bureaus, divisions, and services. Appointments to many of these politically sensitive positions are made on recommendation by department or
(25) agency heads, but all are presumably responsible to Presidential leadership.

One qualification for office at this level is that there be no basic disagreement with Presidential political philosophy, at least so far as administrative judgments and actions are concerned. Apart from
(30) the bi-partisan boards and commissions, these men are normally identified with the political party of the President, or are sympathetic to it, although there are exceptions.

There are four distinguishable kinds of top Presidential appointees, including:

(35) — Those whom the President selects at the outset to establish immediate and effective control over the government (e.g., Cabinet secretaries, agency heads, his own White House staff and Executive Office Personnel).

— Those selected by department and agency heads in order to
(40)   establish control within their respective organizations (e.g.—
assistant secretaries, deputies, assistants to, and major line
posts in some bureaus and divisions).

— High-level appointees who—though often requiring clearance
through political or interest group channels, or both—must
(45)   have known scientific or technical competence (e.g.—the
Surgeon General, the Commissioner of Education).

— Those named to residual positions traditionally filled on a par-
tisan patronage basis.

These appointees are primarily regarded as policy makers and
(50) overseers of policy execution. In practice, however, they usually
have substantial responsibilities in line management, often requiring a thorough knowledge of substantive agency programs.

1. No complete inventory exists of positions in the three highest
   levels of government service because

   (A) no one has bothered to count them
   (B) computers cannot handle all the data
   (C) separate agency personnel systems are used
   (D) the President has never requested such information
   (E) the Classification Act prohibits such a census

2. Top Presidential appointees have as their central responsibility the

   (A) prevention of politically motivated interference with the
       actions of their agencies
   (B) monitoring of government actions on behalf of the President's
       own political party
   (C) translation of the aims of the administration into practical
       programs
   (D) investigation of charges of corruption within the government
   (E) maintenance of adequate controls over the rate of government
       spending

3. One exception to the general rule that top Presidential appointees must be in agreement with the President's political philosophy may be found in

    (A) most cabinet-level officers
    (B) members of the White House staff
    (C) bipartisan boards and commissions
    (D) those offices filled on a patronage basis
    (E) offices requiring scientific or technical expertise

4. Applicants for Presidential appointments are usually identified with or are members of

    (A) large corporations
    (B) the foreign service
    (C) government bureaus
    (D) academic circles
    (E) the President's political party

5. Richard is a terrible driver. He has had at least five traffic violations in the past year.

    Which of the following can be said about the above claim?

    (A) This is an example of an argument that is directed against the source of the claim rather than the claim itself.
    (B) The statement is fallacious because it contains an illegitimate appeal to authority.
    (C) The above argument obtains its strength from a similarity of two compared situations.
    (D) The argument is built upon an assumption that is not stated but rather is concealed.
    (E) In the above statements, there is a shifting in the meaning of terms, causing a fallacy of ambiguity.

6. The exchange rate is the ruling official rate of exchange of dollars for other currencies. It determines the value of American goods in relation to foreign goods. If the dollar is devalued in terms of other currencies, American exports (which are paid for in dollars) become cheaper to foreigners and American imports (paid for by purchasing foreign currency) become more expensive to holders of dollars.

What conclusion can be drawn from the above?

(A) There are certain disadvantages for the United States economy attached to devaluation.
(B) The prospect of devaluation results in a speculative outflow of funds.
(C) By encouraging exports and discouraging imports, devaluation can improve the American balance of payments.
(D) The difference between imports and exports is called the Trade Gap.
(E) It is possible that inflation neutralizes the beneficial effects of devaluation.

7. <u>Although I calculate that he will be here</u> any minute, I cannot wait much longer for him to arrive.

(A) Although I calculate that he will be here
(B) Although I reckon that he will be here
(C) Because I calculate that he will be here
(D) Although I think that he will be here
(E) Because I am confident that he will be here

8. <u>The fourteen-hour day not only has been reduced</u> to one of ten hours but also, in some lines of work, to one of eight or even six.

(A) The fourteen-hour day not only has been reduced
(B) Not only the fourteen-hour day has been reduced
(C) Not the fourteen-hour day only has been reduced
(D) The fourteen-hour day has not only been reduced
(E) The fourteen-hour day has been reduced not only

9. In the human body, platelets promote blood clotting by clumping together. Aspirin has been found to prevent clotting by making platelets less sticky. Research has now shown that heart attacks and strokes caused by blood clots could be avoided by taking one aspirin a day. Statistics show that the incidence of second heart attacks has been reduced by 21% and overall mortality rates by 15% as a result of taking aspirin.

Unfortunately, the drug has several unpleasant side effects, including nausea, gastric bleeding, and, in severe cases, shock. In children, it has been linked to Reye's Syndrome, a rare, but occasionally fatal, childhood illness.

On balance, however, for men aged 40 and over, an aspirin a day may present an excellent prophylactic measure for a disease that affects 1.5 million Americans yearly and claims the lives of about 540,000.

Which of the following conclusions can most properly be drawn from the information above?

(A) All people should take an aspirin a day to prevent heart attacks.
(B) Painkillers prevent heart attacks.
(C) Smokers can safely continue smoking, provided that they take at least one aspirin a day.
(D) The majority of people suffering second subsequent cardiac arrests could have been saved by taking an aspirin a day.
(E) Aspirin can be used to reduce mortality rates in patients who have already suffered heart attacks.

10. In the past, to run for one's country in the Olympics was the ultimate achievement of any athlete. Nowadays, an athlete's motives are more and more influenced by financial gain, and consequently we do not see our best athletes in the Olympics, which is still only for amateurs.

    Which of the following will most weaken the above conclusion?

    (A) The publicity and fame that can be achieved by competing in the Olympics makes athletes more "marketable" by agents and potential sponsors, while allowing the athletes to retain their amateur status.
    (B) The winning of a race is not as important as participating.
    (C) There is a widely held belief that our best Olympic athletes already receive enough in terms of promotion and sponsorship.
    (D) It has been suggested that professional athletes should be allowed to compete in the games.
    (E) Athletics as an entertainment is like any other entertainment job and deserves a financial reward.

11. We want the teacher to be him who has the best rapport with the students.

    (A) We want the teacher to be him
    (B) We want the teacher to be he
    (C) We want him to be the teacher
    (D) We desire that the teacher be him
    (E) We anticipate that the teacher will be him

12. If she were to win the medal, I for one would be disturbed.

    (A) If she were to win the medal,
    (B) If she was to win the medal,
    (C) If she wins the medal,
    (D) If she is the winner of the medal,
    (E) In the event that she wins the medal,

13. The function of a food technologist in a large marketing chain of food stores is to ensure that all foodstuffs which are offered for sale in the various retail outlets meet certain standard criteria for nonperishability, freshness, and fitness for human consumption.

    It is the technologist's job to visit the premises of suppliers and food producers (factory or farm), inspect the facilities and report thereon. Her responsibility also includes receiving new products from local and foreign suppliers and performing exhaustive quality control testing on them. Finally, she should carry out surprise spot-checks on goods held in the marketing chain's own warehouses and stores.

    What conclusion can best be drawn from the preceding paragraph?

    (A) A university degree in food technology is a necessary and sufficient condition for becoming a food technologist.

    (B) Imported products, as well as home-produced goods, must be rigorously tested.

    (C) The food technologist stands between the unhygienic producer and the unsuspecting consumer.

    (D) Home-produced foodstuffs are safer to eat than goods imported from abroad because they are subject to more regular and closer inspection procedures.

    (E) Random checking of the quality of goods stored on the shelves in a foodstore is the best way of ensuring that foodstuffs of an inferior quality are not purchased by the general public.

14. The scouts were told <u>to take an overnight hike, pitch camp, prepare dinner, and that they should be in bed by 9 P.M.</u>

    (A) to take an overnight hike, pitch camp, prepare dinner, and that they should be in bed by 9 P.M.

    (B) to take an overnight hike, to pitch camp, to prepare dinner, and that they should be in bed by 9 P.M.

    (C) to take an overnight hike, pitch camp, prepare dinner, and be in bed by 9 P.M.

    (D) to take an overnight hike, pitching camp, preparing dinner and going to bed by 9 P.M.

    (E) to engage in an overnight hike, pitch camp, prepare dinner, and that they should be in bed by 9 P.M.

Questions 15–18 are based on the following passage.

In the past, American colleges and universities were created to serve a dual purpose—to advance learning and to offer a chance to become familiar with bodies of knowledge already discovered to those who wished it. To create and to impart, these were the hall-
(5) marks of American higher education prior to the most recent, tumultuous decades of the twentieth century. The successful insti-tution of higher learning had never been one whose mission could be defined in terms of providing vocational skills or as a strategy for resolving societal problems. In a subtle way Americans believed
(10) postsecondary education to be useful, but not necessarily of imme-diate use. What the student obtained in college became beneficial in later life—residually, without direct application in the period after graduation.

Another purpose has now been assigned to the mission of
(15) American colleges and universities. Institutions of higher learn-ing—public or private—commonly face the challenge of defining their programs in such a way as to contribute to the service of the community.

One need only be reminded of the change in language describ-
(20) ing the two-year college to appreciate the new value currently being attached to the concept of a service-related university. The tradi-tional two-year college has shed its pejorative "junior" college label and is generally called a "community" college, a clearly value-laden expression representing the latest commitment in higher education.

(25)   This novel development is often overlooked. Educators have always been familiar with those parts of the two-year college cur-riculum that have a "service" or vocational orientation. Knowing this, otherwise perceptive commentaries on American postsec-ondary education underplay the impact of the attempt of colleges
(30) and universities to relate to, if not resolve, the problems of society. Whether the subject under review is student unrest, faculty tenure, the nature of the curriculum, the onset of collective bargaining, or the growth of collegiate bureaucracies, in each instance the thrust of these discussions obscures the larger meaning of the emergence
(35) of the service-university in American higher education. Even the highly regarded critique of Clark Kerr, formerly head of the Carnegie Foundation, which set the parameters of academic debate around the evolution of the so-called "multiversity," failed to take account of this phenomenon.

(40)   Taken together the attrition rate (from known and unknown causes) was 48 percent, but the figure for regular students was 36 percent while for Open Admissions categories it was 56 percent. The most important statistics, however, relate to the findings regarding Open Admissions students, and these indicated as a pro-
(45) jection that perhaps as many as 70 percent would not graduate from a unit of the City University.

15. The dropout rate among regular students in Open Admissions was approximately

    (A) 35%
    (B) 45%
    (C) 55%
    (D) 65%
    (E) 75%

16. According to the passage, in the past it was *not* the purpose of American higher education to

    (A) advance learning
    (B) solve societal problems
    (C) impart knowledge
    (D) train workers
    (E) prepare future managers

17. One of the recent, important changes in higher education relates to

    (A) student representation on college boards
    (B) faculty tenure requirements
    (C) curriculum updates
    (D) service-education concepts
    (E) cost constraints

18. The attrition rate for Open Admissions students was greater than the rate for regular students by what percent?

    (A) 10%
    (B) 20%
    (C) 36%
    (D) 40%
    (E) 46%

19. The <u>government's failing to keep it's pledges</u> will earn the distrust of all the other nations in the alliance.

    (A) government's failing to keep it's pledges
    (B) government failing to keep it's pledges
    (C) government's failing to keep its pledges
    (D) government failing to keep its pledges
    (E) governments failing to keep their pledges

20. Most students like to read <u>these kind of books</u> during their spare time.

    (A) these kind of books
    (B) these kind of book
    (C) this kind of book
    (D) this kinds of books
    (E) those kind of books

21. In the normal course of events, <u>John will graduate high school and enter</u> college in two years.

    (A) John will graduate high school and enter
    (B) John will graduate from high school and enter
    (C) John will be graduated from high school and enter
    (D) John will be graduated from high school and enter into
    (E) John will have graduated high school and enter

22. The daily journey from his home to his office takes John Bond on average an hour and 35 minutes by car. A friend has told him of a different route that is longer in mileage, but will only take an hour and a quarter on average, because it contains stretches of roads where it is possible to drive at higher speeds.

    John Bond's only consideration apart from the time factor is the cost, and he calculates that his car will consume 10% less gasoline if he takes the suggested new route. John decides to take the new route for the next two weeks as an experiment.

    If the above were the only other considerations, which one of the following may have an effect on the decision John has made?

    (A) Major road work is begun on the shorter (in distance) route, which holds up traffic for an extra 10 minutes. The project will take six months, but after it, the improvements will allow the journey to be made in half an hour less than at present.
    (B) There is to be a strike at local gas stations and the amount of gasoline drivers may purchase may be rationed.
    (C) John finds a third route which is slightly longer then his old route, but shorter than the suggested route.
    (D) The old route passes the door of a work colleague, who without a ride, would have to go to work by bus.
    (E) None of the above.

23. All elephants are gray.
    And all mice are gray.
    Therefore, I conclude that all elephants are mice.

    The argument above is invalid because

    (A) the writer bases her argument on another argument that contains circular reasoning.
    (B) the writer has illogically classified two disparate groups together when there is no relationship between them, except that they both have the same attribute.
    (C) the writer has made a mistaken analogy between two dissimilar qualities.
    (D) the writer has used a fallacy which involves the ambiguous description of animals by their color.
    (E) the writer has failed to express her reasoning fully.

24. Sally overslept. Therefore, she did not eat breakfast. She realized that she was late for school, so she ran as fast as she could and did not see a hole in the ground which was in her path. She tripped and broke her ankle. She was then taken to the hospital and while lying in bed was visited by her friend, who wanted to know why she had got up so late.

Which of the following conclusions can be made from the above passage?

(A) Because Sally did not eat her breakfast, she broke her ankle.
(B) Sally's friend visited her in the hospital because she wanted to know why she was late for school.
(C) Sally did not notice the hole because she overslept.
(D) Sally broke her ankle because she went to bed late the previous night.
(E) Sally's broken ankle meant she did not go to school that day.

Questions 25–30 are based on the following passage.

For those of a certain age and educational background, it is hard to think of higher education without thinking of ancient institutions. Some universities are a venerable age—the University of Bologna was founded in 1088 and Oxford University in 1096—and many of
(5) them have a strong sense of tradition. The truly old ones make the most of their pedigrees, and those of a more recent vintage work hard to create an aura of antiquity.

And yet these tradition-loving (or -creating) institutions are currently ending a thunderstorm of changes so fundamental that some
(10) say the very idea of the university is being challenged. Universities are experimenting with new ways of funding (most notably through student fees), forging partnerships with private companies, and engaging in mergers and acquisitions. Such changes are tugging at the ivy's roots.

(15) This is happening for four reasons. The first is the democratization of higher education—"massification," in the language of the educational profession. In the rich world, massification has been going on for some time. The proportion of adults with higher educational qualifications in the OECD countries almost doubled
(20) between 1975 and 2000, from 22 percent to 41 percent. But most

of the rich countries are still struggling to digest this huge growth in numbers. And now massification is spreading to the developing world. China doubled its student population in the late 1990s, and India is trying to follow suit.

(25) The second reason is the rise of the knowledge economy. The world is in the grips of a "soft revolution" in which knowledge is replacing physical resources as the main driver of economic growth. The OECD calculates that between 1985 and 1997, the contribution of knowledge-based industries to total value added *(30)* increased from 51 percent to 59 percent in Germany and from 45 percent to 51 percent in Britain. The best companies are now devoting at least a third of their investment to knowledge-intensive intangibles, such as R&D, licensing, and marketing. Universities are among the most important engines of the knowledge economy. Not *(35)* only do they produce the brain workers who man it, they also provide much of its backbone, from laboratories to libraries to computer networks.

The third factor is globalization. The death of distance is transforming academia just as radically as it is transforming business. *(40)* The number of people from OECD countries studying abroad has doubled over the past 20 years, to 1.9 million; universities are opening campuses all around the world; and a growing number of countries are trying to turn higher education into an export industry.

The fourth is competition. Traditional universities are being *(45)* forced to compete for students and research grants, and private companies are trying to break into a sector that they regard as "the new health care." The World Bank calculates that global spending on higher education amounts to $300 billion a year, or 1 percent of global economic output. There are more than 80 million students *(50)* worldwide, and 3.5 million people are employed to teach them or look after them.

25. Changes in tradition-oriented universities' education are caused by

(A) increased enrollments
(B) lack of financing
(C) online education
(D) more qualified students
(E) lack of resources

26. The best possible title for the passage would be

    (A) *"Massification"*
    (B) *"The Brains Business"*
    (C) *"The Decline of Tradition-Loving Universities"*
    (D) *"Downfall of Academic Dogma"*
    (E) *"Globalization of Higher Education"*

27. According to the passage, mass higher education is forcing universities to become

    (A) more democractic
    (B) better managed
    (C) more liberal
    (D) more teaching-oriented
    (E) more competitive

28. Younger universities try to

    (A) compete with older ones
    (B) create an image like that of more traditional ones
    (C) diversify their student bodies
    (D) rely less on outside financing
    (E) diversify income sources

29. Universities have had to reexamine their mission because

    (A) there are more and better-educated high school graduates
    (B) state funding is declining
    (C) state-run universities are being privatized
    (D) good faculty is in short supply
    (E) of the rise in distance learning

30. In business terms, it can be said that higher education has become

    (A) more profitable
    (B) an export industry
    (C) better managed
    (D) bottom line-oriented
    (E) customer-oriented

31. The owners of a local supermarket have decided to make use of three now-redundant checkout counters. They believe that they will attract those customers who lately have been put off by the long checkout lines during the mid-morning and evening rush hours. The owners have concluded that in order to be successful, the increased revenue from existing and added counters will have to be more than the increase in maintenance costs for the added counters.

    The underlying goal of the owners can be summarized thus:

    (A) To improve services to all customers.
    (B) To attract people who have never been to the store.
    (C) To make use of the redundant counters.
    (D) To keep maintenance costs on the added counters as low as possible.
    (E) To increase monthly profits.

32. The cost of housing in many parts of the United States has become so excessive that many young couples, with above-average salaries, can only afford small apartments. Mortgage commitments are so huge that they cannot consider the possibility of starting a family. A new baby would probably mean either the mother or father giving up a well-paid position. The lack of or great cost of child-care facilities precludes the return of both parents to work.

    Which of the following adjustments could practically be made to the situation described above which would allow young couples to improve their housing prospects?

    (A) Encourage couples to remain childless.
    (B) Encourage couples to have one child only.
    (C) Encourage couples to postpone starting their families until a later age than previously acceptable to society.
    (D) Encourage young couples to move to cheaper areas of the United States.
    (E) Encourage fathers to remain at home while mothers return to work.

33. With the exception of <u>Frank and I, everyone in the class finished</u> the assignment before the bell rang.

    (A) Frank and I, everyone in the class finished
    (B) Frank and me, everyone in the class finished
    (C) Frank and me, everyone in the class had finished
    (D) Frank and I, everyone in the class had finished
    (E) Frank and me everyone in the class finished

34. Many middle-class individuals find that they cannot obtain good medical attention, <u>despite they need it badly.</u>

    (A) despite they need it badly
    (B) despite they badly need it
    (C) in spite of they need it badly
    (D) however much they need it
    (E) therefore, they need it badly

35. Unless new reserves are found soon, the world's supply of coal is being depleted in such a way that with demand continuing to grow at present rates, reserves will be exhausted by the year 2050.

    Which of the following, if true, will most weaken the above argument?

    (A) There has been a slowdown in the rate of increase in world demand for coal over the last 5 years from 10% to 5%.
    (B) It has been known for many years that there are vast stocks of coal under Antarctica which have yet to be economically exploited.
    (C) Oil is being used increasingly in place of coal for many industrial and domestic uses.
    (D) As coal resources are depleted more and more marginal supplies, which are more costly to produce and less efficient in use are being mined.
    (E) None of the above.

36. In accordance with their powers, many state authorities are introducing fluoridation of drinking water. This follows the conclusion of 10 years of research that the process ensures that children and adults receive the required intake of fluoride that will strengthen teeth. The maximum level has been set at one part per million. However, there are many who object, claiming that fluoridation removes freedom of choice.

    Which of the following will weaken the claim of the proponents of fluoridation?

    (A) Fluoridation over a certain prescribed level has been shown to lead to a general weakening of teeth.
    (B) There is no record of the long-term effects of drinking fluoridated water.
    (C) The people to be affected by fluoridation claim that they have not had sufficient opportunity to voice their views.
    (D) Fluoridation is only one part of general dental health.
    (E) Water already contains natural fluoride.

37. When one eats in this restaurant, you often find that the prices are high and that the food is poorly prepared.

    (A) When one eats in this restaurant, you often find
    (B) When you eat in this restaurant, one often finds
    (C) As you eat in this restaurant, you often find
    (D) If you eat in this restaurant, you often find
    (E) When one ate in this restaurant, he often found

38. Ever since the bombing, there has been much opposition from they who maintain that it was an unauthorized war.

    (A) from they who maintain that it was an unauthorized war
    (B) from they who maintain that it had been an unauthorized war
    (C) from those who maintain that it was an unauthorized war
    (D) from they maintaining that it was unauthorized
    (E) from they maintaining that it had been unauthorized

39. <u>I am not to eager to go to this play because it did not get good reviews.</u>

    (A) I am not to eager to go to this play because it did not get good reviews.
    (B) Because of its poor reviews, I am not to eager to go to this play.
    (C) Because of its poor revues, I am not to eager to go to this play.
    (D) I am not to eager to go to this play because the critics did not give it good reviews.
    (E) I am not too eager to go to this play because of its poor reviews.

40. In 1980, global service exports totaled about $370 billion, approximately 20 percent of world trade. Still, no coherent system of rules, principles, and procedures exists to govern trade in services.

    Which of the following best summarizes the argument?

    (A) Regulatory systems lag behind reality.
    (B) A regulatory system ought to reflect the importance of service exports.
    (C) World trade totaled $1850 billion in 1980.
    (D) Service trade legislation is a veritable wasteland.
    (E) While trade legislation exists, it is uncoordinated.

41. <u>It was decided by us that the emphasis would be placed on the results that might be attained.</u>

    (A) It was decided by us that the emphasis would be placed on the results that might be attained.
    (B) We decided that the emphasis would be placed on the results that might be attained.
    (C) We decided to emphasize the results that might be attained.
    (D) We decided to emphasize the results we might attain.
    (E) It was decided that we would place emphasis on the results that might be attained.

IF THERE IS STILL TIME REMAINING, YOU MAY REVIEW YOUR ANSWER. AFTER YOU HAVE CONFIRMED YOUR ANSWER, YOU CANNOT RETURN TO THIS QUESTION.

ANSWER KEY

SAMPLE TEST 2

Quantitative Section

1. C	11. D	21. B	31. C
2. D	12. B	22. C	32. D
3. B	13. A	23. B	33. B
4. E	14. B	24. D	34. D
5. C	15. D	25. A	35. C
6. B	16. A	26. E	36. E
7. C	17. C	27. B	37. A
8. D	18. B	28. E	
9. A	19. E	29. E	
10. B	20. C	30. A	

Verbal Section

1. C	12. A	23. B	34. D
2. C	13. C	24. C	35. E
3. C	14. C	25. D	36. B
4. E	15. A	26. B	37. C
5. D	16. B	27. E	38. C
6. C	17. D	28. B	39. E
7. D	18. B	29. A	40. B
8. E	19. C	30. B	41. C
9. E	20. C	31. E	
10. A	21. B	32. C	
11. B	22. C	33. C	

ANALYSIS

Self-Scoring Guide—Analytical Writing

Evaluate your writing tests (or have a friend or teacher evaluate them for you) on the following basis. Read each essay completely, paying special attention to its logical organization and use of examples and facts to buttress its claims or position. Assign a holistic score between 0 and 6, using the scale below. Your writing score will be the average of the scores of the two essays.

6   **Outstanding:** Cogent, well-articulated analysis of the issue or critique of the argument. Develops a position with insightful reasons and persuasive examples. Well organized. Superior command of language and variety of syntax. Only minor flaws in grammar, usage, and mechanics.

5   **Strong:** Well-developed analysis or critique. Develops a position with well-chosen examples or reasons. Generally well organized. Clear control of language and variety of syntax. Minor flaws in grammar, usage, and mechanics.

4   **Adequate:** Competent analysis or critique. Develops a position with relevant reasons or examples. Adequately organized. Adequate control of language, but may lack syntactic variety. May have some flaws in grammar, usage, and mechanics.

3   **Limited**: Competent but clearly flawed analysis or critique. Vague or limited in developing a position. Poorly organized. Weak in using relevant examples or reasons. Language used imprecisely or lacking in sentence variety. Contains major errors or frequent minor errors in grammar, usage, and mechanics.

2   **Seriously Flawed**: Serious weaknesses in analysis and organization. Unclear or seriously limited in presenting or developing a position. Disorganized. Few relevant examples or reasons. Frequent serious problems in language and sentence structure. Numerous errors in grammar, usage, or mechanics that interfere with meaning.

1   **Fundamentally Deficient**: Little evidence of ability to organize and develop a coherent response to issue or argument. Severe and persistent errors in language and sentence structure. Pervasive pattern of errors in grammar, usage, and mechanics that severely interfere with meaning.

0   **Unscorable**: Illegible or not written in the assigned topic.

ANSWERS EXPLAINED

Quantitative Section

1. **(C)**

Difficulty Level

The volume of water that has been poured into the tank is 5 cubic feet per minute for 6 minutes, or 30 cubic feet. The tank is rectangular, so its volume is length times width times height, with the answer in cubic units. The width is $\frac{1}{2}$ the length, or $\frac{1}{2}$ of 4 feet which is 2 feet.

The volume, which we already know is 30 cubic feet, is, therefore, 4 feet × 2 feet × the height. The height (depth of the water in the tank) is, therefore, $\frac{30}{8} = 3\frac{3}{4}$ feet = 3 feet 9 inches.

2. **(D)**

Difficulty Level

Since −3 has the largest absolute value of the three given numbers, using z as −3 will make z^2 as large as possible. Since $\frac{x}{y}$ is a quotient, to make it as large as possible use the smallest positive number for y and the largest positive number for x. So if you use $x = 2$ and $y = \frac{1}{2}$, then $\frac{x}{y}$ is as large as possible. Therefore, the largest value of the expression is $\frac{2}{\frac{1}{2}}(-3)^2 = 4(9) = 36$.

3. **(B)**

Difficulty Level

The total number of people surveyed was $n + x$. Since 70 percent of the total preferred brand A, that means $.7(n + x)$ preferred brand A. However, 60 percent of the n people and all of the x people preferred brand A. So $.6n + x$ preferred brand A. Therefore, $.7(n + x)$ must equal $.6n + x$. So we have $.7n + .7x = .6n + x$. Solving for x gives $0.1n = 0.3x$ or $x = \frac{n}{3}$.

4. **(E)**

6
Difficulty Level

Since STATEMENT (1) describes only x and STATEMENT (2) describes only y, both are needed to get an answer. Using STATEMENT (2), STATEMENT (1) becomes $3x = 2k = 2y^2$, so $x = \frac{2}{3}y^2$. However, this is not sufficient since if $y = -1$, then $x = \frac{2}{3}$ and x is greater than y, but if $y = 1$, then again $x = \frac{2}{3}$ but now x is less than y.

Therefore, STATEMENTS (1) and (2) together are not sufficient.

5. **(C)**

4
Difficulty Level

$ABCD$ is a parallelogram if AB is parallel to CD and BC is parallel to AD. STATEMENT (2) tells you that AB is parallel to CD, but this is not sufficient since a trapezoid has only one pair of opposite sides parallel. Thus, STATEMENT (2) alone is not sufficient.

STATEMENT (1) alone is not sufficient since a trapezoid can have the two nonparallel sides equal.

However, using STATEMENTS (1) and (2) together we can deduce that BC is parallel to AD since the distance from BC to AD is equal along two different parallel lines.

6. **(B)**

9
Difficulty Level

A diagram always helps. You are given that BC and EF are each 2 feet. Since the area of a rectangle is length times width, you must find the length (CE or BF). Look at the triangle ABF. It has two equal sides ($AB = AF$), so the perpendicular from A to the line BF divides ABF into two congruent right triangles, AHF and AHB, each with hypotenuse 2.

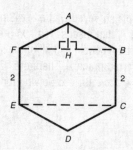

The angle *FAB* is 120° since the total of all the angles of the hexagon is 720°. So each of the two triangles is a 30° – 60° – 90° right triangle with hypotenuse 2. So *AH* = 1, and *FH* and *HB* must equal $\sqrt{3}$. Therefore, *BF* is $2\sqrt{3}$ and the area is $2 \times 2\sqrt{3} = 4\sqrt{3}$ square feet.

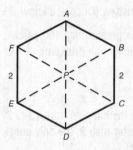

(You can find the sum of the angles of any convex polygon by connecting all vertices to a fixed interior point, *P*. In the case of the hexagon this will give 6 triangles. The total of all the triangles' angles is $6 \times 180° = 1,080°$. Since the angles at the fixed point, which are not part of the hexagon angles, will add up to 360°, the sum of the hexagon's angles is $1,080° – 360° = 720°$.)

7. **(C)**   **6**

Difficulty Level

You want the ratio of the percentage who own both a car and a motorcycle to the percentage who own a motorcycle. You know that 15 percent own a motorcycle, so you need to find the percentage who own both a car and a motorcycle. Let *A* stand for the percentage who own both a car and a motorcycle. Then (the percentage who own a car) plus (the percentage who own a motorcycle) minus *A* must equal the percentage who own one or the other or both. Since 100 percent own one or the other or both, we obtain $90\% + 15\% – A = 105\% – A = 100\%$. So *A* = 5%. Since 15 percent own motorcycles, the percentage of motorcycle owners who own cars is $\frac{5\%}{15\%} = \frac{1}{3} = 33\frac{1}{3}\%$.

8. **(D)**   **7**

Difficulty Level

To do computations, change percentages to decimals. Let *J, M, B,* and *L* stand for Jim's, Marcia's, Bob's, and Lee's respective weights. Then we know $J = 1.4M$, $B = .9L$, and $L = 2M$. We need to know *B* as a percentage of *J*. Since $B = .9L$ and $L = 2M$, we have $B = .9(2M) = 1.8M$.

$J = 1.4M$ is equivalent to $M = \left(\dfrac{1}{1.4}\right)J$. So $B = 1.8M = 1.8\left(\dfrac{1}{1.4}\right)J =$
$\left(\dfrac{9}{7}\right)J$. Converting to a percentage, we have $\dfrac{9}{7} = 1.28\left(\dfrac{4}{7}\right) = 128\dfrac{4}{7}\%$,
so (D) is the correct answer. (Once you know $B = \dfrac{9}{7}J$, this means the
correct answer must be greater than 100 percent so you should guess
(D) or (E) if you can't finish the problem).

9. **(A)**

Difficulty Level

Two-digit numbers are the integers from 10 to 99. Since you are told
that the number is greater than 9, the only possible choices are
integers 10, 11, . . ., 99.

STATEMENT (1) alone is sufficient since (1) is equivalent to $9a = b$. In
this case if a is greater than 1, then $9a$ is not a digit, and if a is 0, then
the number is not greater than 9. Thus there is only one possible
choice, $a = 1$, which yields the number 19, which satisfies (1).

STATEMENT (2) alone is not sufficient since 19, 38, 57, 76, and 95
satisfy (2) and are two-digit numbers greater than 9.

So (A) is the correct choice.

10. **(B)**

Difficulty Level

Since 108 percent of $50 = (1.08)(50) = \$54$, the chair was offered
for sale at $54.00. It was sold for 90 percent of $54 since there was a
10 percent discount. Therefore, the chair was sold for $(.9)(\$54)$ or
$48.60.

11. **(D)**

Difficulty Level

k is a prime if none of the integers 2, 3, 4, . . . up to $k-1$ divide k
evenly. STATEMENT (1) alone is sufficient since if k is not a prime, then
$k = (m)(n)$, where m and n must be integers less than k. But this means
either m or n must be less than or equal to $\sqrt{k}$ since if m and n are
both larger than $\sqrt{k}$, $(m)(n)$ is larger than $\left(\sqrt{k}\right)\left(\sqrt{k}\right)$ or k. So
STATEMENT (1) implies k is a prime.

STATEMENT (2) alone is also sufficient since if $k = (m)(n)$ and m and
n are both larger than $\dfrac{k}{2}$, then $(m)(n)$ is greater than $\dfrac{k^2}{4}$, but $\dfrac{k^2}{4}$ is

greater than k when k is larger than 5. Therefore, if no integer between 2 and $\dfrac{k}{2}$, inclusive divides k evenly, then k is a prime.

12. **(B)** 🎯 6
Difficulty Level

The towns can be thought of as the vertices of a triangle.

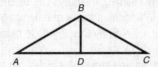

Since the distance from A to B is equal to the distance from B to C, the triangle is isosceles. The point D on AC that is closest to B is the point on AC such that BD is perpendicular to AC. (If BD were not perpendicular to AC, then there would be a point on AC closer to B than D; in the diagram, E is closer to B than D is.)

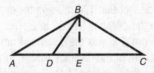

So the triangles ABD and CBD are right triangles with two corresponding sides equal. Therefore, ABD is congruent to CBD. Thus, $AD = DC$, and since AC is 60, AD must be 30. Since ABD is a right triangle with hypotenuse 50 and another side equal to 30, the remaining side (BD) must be 40.

13. **(A)** 🎯 5
Difficulty Level

Here's a table of the hours worked:

	Mon.	Tues.	Wed.	Thurs.	Fri.	Wages for week
Hours worked	8	8	8	8	8	$5x$
Excess worked over 8 hr	0	3	1	2	1	$(0 + 3 + 1 + 2 + 1)y = 7y$

The average daily wage equals $\dfrac{(5x + 7y)}{5}$ or $x + \dfrac{7}{5}y = x + 1.4y.$

14. **(B)**

8
Difficulty Level

There are 8 choices for the first female, then 7 choices for the second female, and 6 choices for the third female on the committee. So there are $8 \times 7 \times 6$ different ways to pick the 3 females in order. However, if member A is chosen first, then member B, and then member C, the same 3 females are chosen as when C is followed by A and B is chosen last. In fact, the same 3 members can be chosen in $3 \times 2 \times 1$ different orders. So to find the number of different groups of 3 females, DIVIDE $(8 \times 7 \times 6)$ by $(3 \times 2 \times 1)$ to obtain 56.

In the same way, there are $8 \times 7 \times 6 = 336$ ways to choose the 3 males in order, but any group of 3 males can be put in order $3 \times 2 \times 1 = 6$ different ways. So there are $\frac{336}{6} = 56$ different groups of 3 males. Therefore, there are $56 \times 56 = 3{,}136$ different committees.

15. **(D)**

4
Difficulty Level

Since we are given the fact that 100 miles is the distance from A to B, it is sufficient to find the distance from C to B. This is so because 100 minus the distance from C to B is the distance from A to C. STATEMENT (1) says that 125 percent of the distance from C to B is 100 miles. Thus, we can find the distance from C to B, which is sufficient. Since the distance from A to C plus the distance from C to B is the distance from A to B, we can use STATEMENT (2) to set up the equation 5 times the distance from A to C equals 100 miles.

Therefore, STATEMENTS (1) and (2) are each sufficient.

16. **(A)**

5
Difficulty Level

Each member has a $\frac{1}{15}$ chance to be the first one picked. So the probability that the first person picked is female is $\frac{5}{15}$. If the first person picked is female, then there are 14 tickets left in the box with only 4 female members of the club left. So the probability that the second person picked is female if the first person picked was female is $\frac{4}{14}$. In order for both persons to be female, the first person must be female and then the second person must be female, so the probability that both persons are female is $\left(\frac{5}{15} \right)\left(\frac{4}{14} \right) = \frac{2}{21}$.

Another method of solving the problem follows. The number of ways the 2 tickets can be picked in order is 15×14, and the number of ways 2 females can be picked in order is 5×4. So the probability that both persons picked are female is $\left(\dfrac{5 \times 4}{15 \times 14}\right) = \left(\dfrac{1}{2}\right)\left(\dfrac{2}{7}\right) = \dfrac{2}{21}$.

17. (C)

Difficulty Level **4**

Since the standard deviation is 5 percent, 2 standard deviations is 10 percent. The mean is 82 percent, so the score that is 2 standard deviations above the mean is 82% + 10% = 92 percent. Notice that this problem really has nothing to do with statistics because all you need to do is plug in the values.

18. (B)

Difficulty Level **5**

STATEMENT (2) alone is sufficient since $x = y$ implies $x - y = 0$.

STATEMENT (1) alone is not sufficient. An infinite number of pairs satisfy STATEMENT (1), for example, $x = 2$, $y = 2$, for which $x - y = 0$, and $x = 4$, $y = 1$, for which $x - y = 3$.

19. (E)

Difficulty Level **6**

Since there is no information on how many of the eligible voters are men or how many are women, STATEMENTS (1) and (2) together are not sufficient.

20. (C)

Difficulty Level **5**

Let x_n be what the motorcycle is worth after n years. Then we know $x_0 = \$2,500$ and $x_{n+1} = .8x_n$. So $x_1 = .8 \times 2,500$, which is \$2,000. x_2 is $.8 \times 2,000$, which is 1,600, and finally x_3 is $.8 \times 1,600$, which is 1,280. Therefore, the motorcycle is worth \$1,280 at the end of three years *or* $x_3 = .8x_2 = .8(.8x_1) = .8(.8)(.8 \, x_0) = .512 \times 2,500 = 1,280$.

21. (B)

Difficulty Level **5**

Simply use the properties of inequalities to solve the given inequality. Subtract $12x$ from each side to get $-5x - 5 < 18$. Next add 5 to each side to obtain $-5x < 23$. Finally, divide each side by -5 to get $x > -23/5$. Remember that if you divide each side of an inequality by a negative number, the inequality is reversed. You can make a quick check of your answer by using $x = -5$, which is not greater than $-\dfrac{23}{5}$, and $x = -4$, which is greater than $-\dfrac{23}{5}$ in the original inequality. Since $x = -5$ does not satisfy the original inequality (-40 is not less than -42) and $x = -4$ does satisfy the inequality (-33 is less than -30), the answer is correct. You could use the method of checking values to find the correct answer, but it would take longer.

22. **(C)**

Difficulty Level

Draw the radii from O to each of the vertices. These lines divide the hexagon into six triangles. STATEMENT (2) says that all the triangles are congruent since each of their pairs of corresponding sides is equal. Since there are 360° in a circle, the central angle of each triangle is 60°. And, since all radii are equal, each angle of the triangle equals 60°. Therefore, the triangles are equilateral, and AB is equal to the radius of the circle. Thus, if we assume STATEMENT (1), we know the length of AB. Without STATEMENT (1), we can't find the length of AB.

Also, STATEMENT (1) alone is not sufficient since AB need not equal the radius unless the hexagon is regular.

23. **(B)**

Difficulty Level

STATEMENT (2) alone is sufficient. If (2) holds, then $\dfrac{32}{(32 + 5{,}678)}$ represents the ratio of defective items to total items produced. Since any fraction can be changed into a percentage by multiplying by 100, STATEMENT (2) alone is sufficient.

STATEMENT (1) alone is not sufficient since the total number of items produced is also needed to find the percentage of defective items.

Therefore, (B) is the correct choice.

24. **(D)**

Difficulty Level

Since 20 was added to each age, the mean of the listed ages will be 20 more than the mean of the actual ages. [Note that this means you can eliminate (B), (C), and (E) and that you should guess (A) or (D) if you can't solve the problem.] The standard deviation and the range of a list measure how spread out the data is; adding the same number to every measurement in the list will not change either of these, so the correct answer is (D).

25. **(A)**

Difficulty Level

STATEMENT (1) alone is sufficient. Since $3^2 + 4^2 = 5^2$, ABC is a right triangle by the Pythagorean theorem.

STATEMENT (2) alone is not sufficient since you can choose a point D so that $AC = CD$ for *any* triangle ABC.

26. **(E)**

Difficulty Level

(1) and (2) are not sufficient. The price of food could rise for other reasons besides the price of energy rising.

27. **(B)**

Difficulty Level

Let M, J, and K be the amounts paid by Mary, John, and Karen, respectively. Then $K = 1.5J$, $M = \left(\dfrac{5}{6}\right)K$, and $M = J + 2$. So M, which is $\dfrac{5}{6}K$, must be $\left(\dfrac{5}{6}\right)(1.5)J = \left(\dfrac{5}{6}\right)\left(\dfrac{3}{2}\right)J = \dfrac{5}{4}J$. Therefore, we have $\left(\dfrac{5}{4}\right)J = J + 2$ or $\left(\dfrac{1}{4}\right)J = 2$, which means $J = 8$. So $K = 1.5J$, or 12, and $M = J + 2$, or 10. So the total is $8 + 12 + 10 = \$30$.

28. **(E)**

Difficulty Level

The number who subscribed to at least one magazine is the sum of the numbers who subscribed to exactly one, two, and three magazines. So $38 = N1 + N2 + N3$, where $N1$, $N2$, and $N3$ are the number who subscribed to 1, 2, and 3 magazines, respectively. We need to find $N2$. STATEMENT (1) is not sufficient since it gives the value of $N3$ but $N1$ and $N2$ are still both unknown. Even if we also use STATEMENT (1), we cannot find $N2$ since we have no information about the number of subscribers to magazines B and C.

29. **(E)**

Difficulty Level

STATEMENT (1) is insufficient since 9 (which is odd) and 6 (which is even) are both divisible by 3.

STATEMENT (2) is also insufficient since $\sqrt{81}$ and $\sqrt{36}$ are both divisible by 3. Both 81 and 36 are divisible by 3, so (1) and (2) together are still insufficient.

30. **(A)**

6
Difficulty Level

The angles are in the ratio 1 : 2 : 2, so two angles are equal to each other and both are twice as large as the third angle of the triangle. Since a triangle with two equal angles must have the sides opposite equal, the triangle is isosceles. (Using the fact that the sum of the angles of a triangle is 180°, you can see that the angles of the triangle are 72°, 72°, and 36°, so only (A) is true.)

31. **(C)**

5
Difficulty Level

(1) alone is obviously insufficient. To use (2) you need to know what the painting was worth at some time between 1988 and 1997. So (2) alone is insufficient, but by using (1) and (2) together you can figure out the worth of the painting in January 1991. NOTE: You should not waste time actually figuring out the value.

32. **(D)**

6
Difficulty Level

(1) alone is sufficient since the rule enables you to compute all successive values once you know a_1. Also, the rule and (1) tell you that the numbers in the sequence will always increase. Thus, since $a_2 = 4$, 3 will never appear. In the same way, by using (2) and the rule for the sequence, you can determine that $a_2 = 4$ and a_1 is 2 or −2, so the reasoning used above shows that 3 will never appear.

33. **(B)**

8
Difficulty Level

The area of the wall is 11 feet × 20 feet = 220 square feet. Since a large roll of wallpaper gives more square feet per dollar, you should try to use large rolls. Since $\frac{220}{60}$ = 3 with a remainder of 40, if you buy 3 large rolls, which cost 3 × $25 = $75, you will have enough to cover the entire wall, except for 40 square feet. You can cover 40 square feet by either buying 1 large roll or 4 small rolls. A large roll costs $25 but 4 small rolls cost only $24. So the minimum cost is $75 + $24 = $99.

34. **(D)**

4
Difficulty Level

If there are x red marbles and y green marbles in the jar, then ($y + 1$) marbles must contain at least one red marble. So it is sufficient to know the number of red marbles and the number of green marbles. Since you are given that $x + y = 60$, STATEMENT (2) is obviously sufficient. Also, STATEMENT (1) is sufficient since it implies that $x = 2y$, which enables you to find x and y. Therefore, the correct answer choice is (D).

35. (C)

Difficulty Level 5

STATEMENT (2) alone is not sufficient. -1 is less than 2, and $\dfrac{1}{-1}$ is less than $\dfrac{1}{2}$, but 1 is less than 2 and $\dfrac{1}{1}$ is greater than $\dfrac{1}{2}$.

STATEMENT (1) alone is insufficient since there is no information about y.

STATEMENT (1) and (2) together imply that x and y are both greater than 1, and for two positive numbers x and y, if x is less than y, then $\dfrac{1}{x}$ is greater than $\dfrac{1}{y}$.

36. (E)

Difficulty Level 6

Since C is closer to A, if plane X is flying faster than plane Y, it will certainly fly over C before plane Y. However, if plane X flies slower than plane Y, and C is very close to A, plane X will still fly over C before plane Y does. Thus, STATEMENTS (1) and (2) together are not sufficient.

37. (A)

Difficulty Level 6

To compare two fractions, the fractions must have the same denominator. The least common denominator for both fractions is 120. Using this fact, $\dfrac{x}{12} = \dfrac{10x}{120}$ and $\dfrac{y}{40} = \dfrac{3y}{120}$. So the relation between the fractions is the same as the relation between $10x$ and $3y$. Therefore, STATEMENT (1) alone is sufficient. STATEMENT (2) alone is not sufficient. Using $y = 13$ and $x = 4$, STATEMENT (2) is true and $\dfrac{x}{12}$ is greater than $\dfrac{y}{40}$. However, using $y = 10$ and $x = 2$, STATEMENT (2) is still true, but now $\dfrac{x}{12}$ is less than $\dfrac{y}{40}$.

Verbal Section

1. **(C)**

Difficulty Level **5**

See paragraph 2.

2. **(C)**

Difficulty Level **6**

See paragraph 3: "Top Presidential appointees, . . . bear the brunt of translating the philosophy and aims of the current administration into practical programs."

3. **(C)**

Difficulty Level **5**

See paragraph 4, sentence 2.

4. **(E)**

Difficulty Level **3**

See paragraph 4, last line.

5. **(D)**

Difficulty Level **7**

Analysis of the two sentences indicates the presence of an assumption that anyone who has had at least five traffic violations in a year is a terrible driver. This assumption is understood but is not stated. Rather, it is a hidden assumption, making (D) the appropriate answer. Alternative (A) is incorrect because there is no attack on the source of the claim. (B) is wrong because there is no appeal to authority— illegitimate or not. (C) is not the correct answer because there is no comparison of two similar situations in the statement. (E) is incorrect because there is no term with a confusing or double meaning.

6. **(C)**

Difficulty Level **4**

The best conclusion that can be drawn from the statement is one that sums up the facts that are given in one sentence; thus, (C) is the best answer. Although the given paragraph states that if there is devaluation of the dollar, American imports will become more expensive, this will not necessarily be a disadvantage for the U.S. economy. Hence, (A) is not appropriate. Alternative (B) is also inappropriate, because it highlights a disadvantage that may arise from the expectation of devaluation, but which is not dealt with in the paragraph. Alternatives (D) and

(E) are both helpful pieces of information, but they cannot be concluded from the given text.

7. **(D)**

Difficulty Level

Do not use *calculate* or *reckon* when you mean *think*.

8. **(E)**

Difficulty Level

Since the words *but also* precede a phrase, to *one of eight or even six*, the words *not only* should precede a phrase, *to one of ten hours*. This error in parallel structure is corrected in choice E.

9. **(E)**

Difficulty Level

According to the passage, all people cannot take aspirin without undesirable side effects, and in some cases, the danger caused by aspirin itself outweighs its benefits. The passage, by saying "On balance, however, for men aged 40 and over, an aspirin a day may present. . . ." also implies that not all, but only some people (men over 40) should take an aspirin a day. Alternative answer (A) clearly cannot be concluded from the passage. Answer alternative (B) is also inappropriate. No painkiller other than aspirin is mentioned in the passage, and it cannot be inferred that all painkillers reduce the "stickiness" of platelets. (C) is incorrect. Smoking is not mentioned in the passage and since studies of the effects of smoking and aspirin have not been reported, no conclusions can be drawn. (D) is wrong because the statistics given in the passage say that 15% of second heart attack victims were saved from death by taking aspirin, and 15% does not constitute a majority. (E) is the correct choice since it simply states that mortality rates can be reduced in patients who have already suffered a heart attack (as stated in the passage), without giving any specific statistics.

10. **(A)**

Difficulty Level

It is fact that athletes can attract sponsorship and make money and that participation in the Olympics can aid this process. On the basis that it is true that athletes are more and more attracted by the profit motive, the conclusion that the best athletes do not compete in the Olympics is weakened. Therefore, A is the appropriate answer. Alternative (B) is an oft-stated maxim, but in this case, it is not relevant to the argument.

The fact that people believe that amateur athletes are receiving adequate alternative remuneration does not bear on the argument for allowing genuine professional athletes into the games. So, (C) is inappropriate. Choice (D) comes close to weakening the argument, because if professional (as well as amateur) athletes were allowed to compete, presuming the participants were selected on merit, then the best athletes would be seen. However, it has only been a suggestion, perhaps in the past, (in which case it was not adopted) or in the future (in which case its adoption is not certain). Choice (E) represents an opinion that might or might not be held by the writer, but, whether or not the author agrees, it does not weaken the argument; therefore (E) is inappropriate.

11. **(B)**

7
Difficulty Level

"He" is the subject of the sentence which takes who as the relative pronoun.

12. **(A)**

4
Difficulty Level

No error.

13. **(C)**

4
Difficulty Level

The paragraph demonstrates from beginning to end that the function of the food technologist is to prevent unfit foodstuffs from being marketed by the stores and passed on to the consumer, who relies on the store's control procedures. (C), therefore, is the most appropriate answer. Answer alternative (A) is inappropriate because it cannot be inferred from the text (even if it were true). Answer (B) and possibly answer (D) are factually correct, but these conclusions cannot be drawn from the text itself. (E) is not a correct interpretation of the facts; random checking is not the best way, since below-standard goods are caught in the net only by chance.

14. **(C)**

7
Difficulty Level

This choice does not violate parallel structure.

15. **(A)**

7
Difficulty Level

The dropout rate on average for all Open Admissions students was 48%; for regular students, 36%; and for Open Admissions categories, 56%.

16. **(B)**
Difficulty Level

See paragraph 1: "The successful institution of higher learning had never been one whose mission could be defined in terms of providing vocational skills or . . . resolving societal problems." This is the sort of question that must be read carefully; it asks for an answer that is not among the alternatives given in the passage.

17. **(D)**
Difficulty Level

The idea that a university must relate to the problems of society is given in paragraph 2.

18. **(B)**
Difficulty Level

The attrition rate for Open Admissions students was 56 percent, and that for regular students 36 percent, a difference of 20 percent.

19. **(C)**
Difficulty Level

Choice C corrects errors in the possessive form of *government* (needed before a verbal noun) and *it*.

20. **(C)**
Difficulty Level

This is also an error in agreement: *Kind* is singular and requires a singular modifier (*this*).

21. **(B)**
Difficulty Level

The correct idiom is *graduate from*. The active case is preferred to the passive used in choice C. Choice D adds an unnecessary word, *into*.

22. **(C)**
Difficulty Level

John's decision is to experiment with the new longer (in mileage) route for two weeks, and it is this decision that we have to consider. Choice (C), by offering a third alternative, gives John another possibility and, therefore, another outcome. It may affect his decision, and therefore, is the appropriate answer. Alternatives (A), (B), and (D) alter factors within the calculation affecting the decision, but taken individually and not making any other changes, will definitely not result in a different decision being made. These three are, therefore, not appropriate answers. The existence of a definite answer—in this case, (C)—means that alternative (E) is not appropriate.

23. **(B)**

6
Difficulty Level

There is only one argument in the passage based on two separate premises upon which the writer has based his conclusion. Choice (A) is inappropriate because there is no other argument. Choice (C) is incorrect because the qualities are the same (gray). (D) is inappropriate because the description is not ambiguous, and (E) is wrong because the writer has stated an argument—albeit invalid.

24. **(C)**

9
Difficulty Level

Here we have a chain of events where the conclusion of one argument becomes the premise for another. Only (C) can be concluded from the facts given in the passage—that is, because Sally overslept she ran toward school, and because she ran, she did not notice the hole. Choice (A) is inappropriate because the chain of events is not linked by the fact that Sally did not eat her breakfast. The passage does not include a consequence emanating from that fact. Choice (B) is not appropriate because there is no way to link Sally's friend to the events in the passage. Similarly, facts not included preclude (D) from being the appropriate answer. Finally, (E) cannot be inferred, as we do not know what Sally did later that day; she may have been released from the hospital and gone to school.

25. **(D)**

8
Difficulty Level

Massification, as it is termed in paragraph 3. While there are increased enrollments (A), these are a function of massification. None of the other alternatives is mentioned.

26. **(B)**

7
Difficulty Level

_passage is about the business of education, or "brains." Alternatives _(E) are mentioned, but they don't touch on the central idea. _ basis for (C) or (D). Oxford University and other tradition-_ _ersities are not in decline. (D) is not mentioned at all.

27. **(E)**

Difficulty Level

Traditional universities are being forced to compete for students (last paragraph). There is no mention of the other alternatives.

28. **(B)**

Difficulty Level

See paragraph 1. The old universities' attempt to maintain their image, whereas younger ones try to "create an aura of antiquity" (paragraph 1). It is true that younger universities compete with older ones, but that is the second-best answer.

29. **(A)**

Difficulty Level

See paragraph 3. There are better-educated high school graduates, forcing universities to undergo change (paragraph 3).

30. **(B)**

Difficulty Level

This answer is given in paragraph 5. One of the major forces for change in higher education is the globalization of the industry. None of the other alternatives is mentioned.

31. **(E)**

Difficulty Level

Services will be improved, it is hoped, for a certain segment of customers—those that shop during the rush hours—but not for all customers. This fact makes choice (A) inappropriate. To attract new customers is not stated in the passage as an objective, so (B) is inappropriate. The utilization of excess capacity, as in (C) is a useful by-product of the new system, but it is not the main goal. If maintenance costs are kept low, it will probably make the achievement of the main goal that much easier, but this is not the major objective so choice (D) is not appropriate. The principal purpose of the owners is to make more money from the change, by increasing income more than the added costs. Therefore, (E) is the appropriate answer.

32. **(C)**

Difficulty Level

Encouraging couples to remain childless would have a negative social effect and would not be practical, so answer alternative (A) is not a reasonable suggestion. The income loss involved in having one child is not much more than that involved in having two or more children (assuming the loss of the income of one parent or the expense of child care), so suggestion (B) is also invalid. If couples move to cheaper areas in the country, as suggested in (D), the chances are that work would be less available or possibly that the couple would have a less positive economic future, so the change may not necessarily be financially advantageous. If fathers stayed at home rather than mothers, there would be no improvement in financial status, so suggestion (E) is invalid. Suggestion (C) is the only sensible solution, since financial stability is likely to increase with the length of time in employment.

33. **(C)**
❹
Difficulty Level

This corrects the two errors in this sentence—the error in case (*me for I*) and the error in tense (*had finished* for *finished*).

34. **(D)**
❽
Difficulty Level

Despite should be used as a preposition, not as a word joining clauses.

35. **(E)**
❽
Difficulty Level

Even if the rate of increase in demand has slowed from 10% per annum to 5% per annum over the last five years, that means that demand is still increasing at 5% per annum. If, as the passage states, demand continues to grow at the present rate—that is, by 5% per annum—the world's resources will be used up by the year 2050. Therefore, the argument is not weakened by the statement in answer alternative (A). Choice (B) introduces the matter of supply, but apparently the reserves in Antarctica have been known for some time, and this, therefore, does not affect the argument that stocks will be depleted unless new reserves are found. Choice (C) informs us that there is an alternative to coal which is being used increasingly. However, the questions of the supply of and the rate of growth of demand for oil do not affect the argument in the paragraph. Choice (D) states an economic fact of life that will have to be faced if the statements in the paragraph are true. It may lead to a search for alternative fuels and consequent decrease in demand for coal, but this is uncertain and cannot be inferred. So, neither (A), (B), (C), or (D) are appropriate. Choice (E) is, therefore, the correct answer.